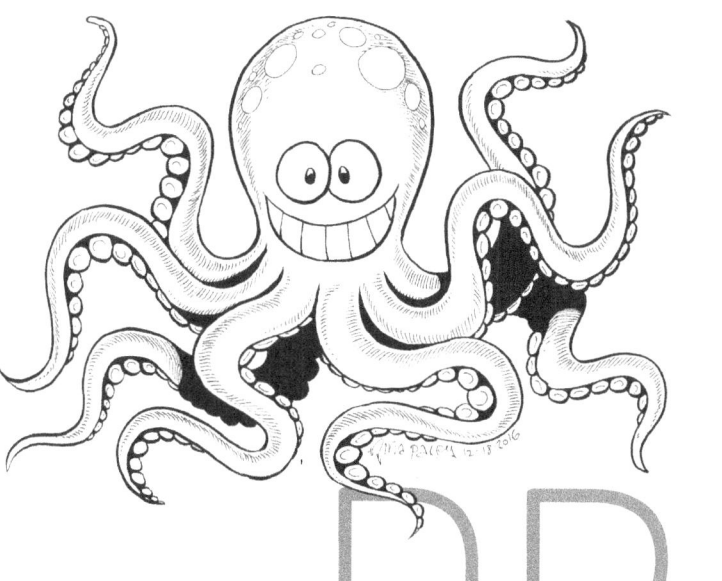

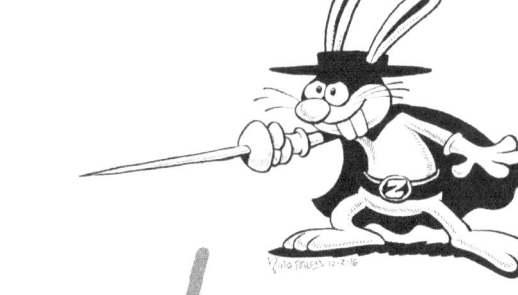

DRAW, MONKEY, DRAW!

A Hundred Dollar Drawing
Adult Coloring Book by Nina Paley

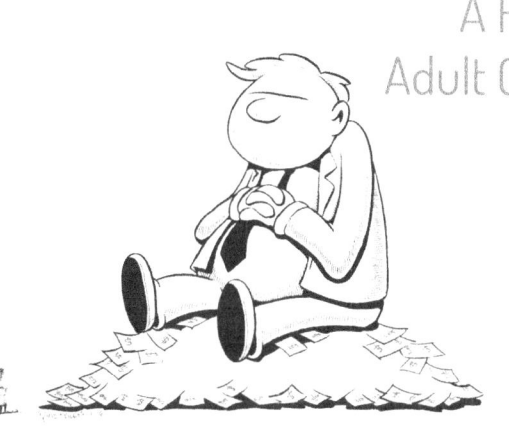
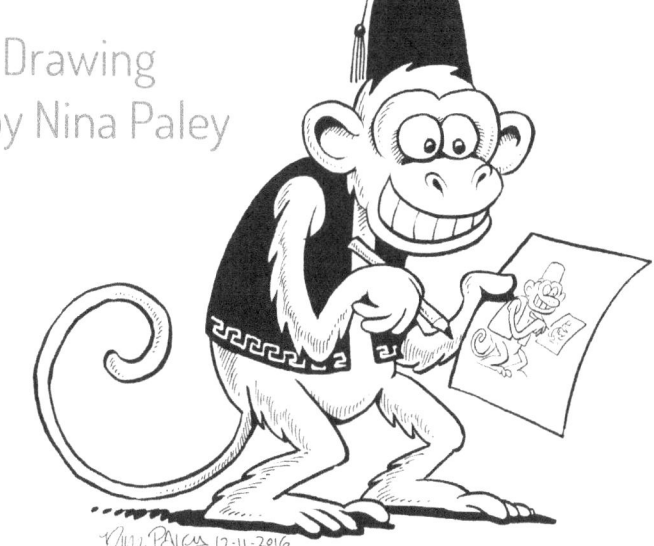

Book Layout Assistance by Matt Wiley

♡2016 by Nina Paley. Copying is an act of love. Please copy and share.
copyheart.org
ninapaley.com

In October 2016 I noticed some artists and animators posting drawings online with the hashtag #inktober. This is the sort of thing I never do, but it had been years since I'd respectfully drawn with ink on paper, and I kind of missed it. So I ordered myself some different brush pens, and the day they arrived I sat down and drew these:

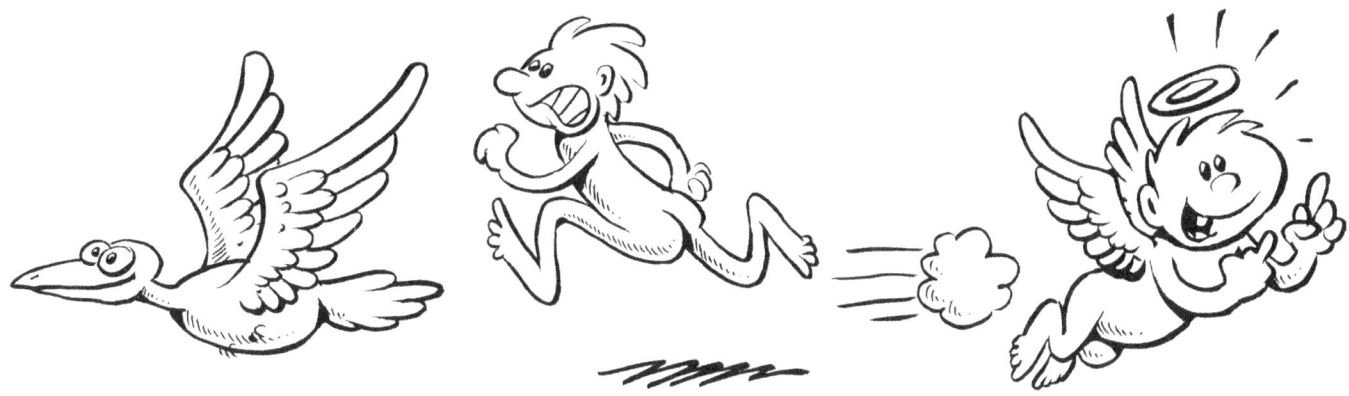

No warm-ups, no practice, just bam, out they came.

It had been more than a decade since I'd drawn in this style, a result of burn-out from drawing daily comic strips. Advice to you kids: turning something you enjoy into a daily job is a great way to make you hate it. I quit my last syndicated comic, The Hots, in 2003. I guess 12 years is enough time to recover from style burn-out, at least a little.

I enjoyed drawing so much, I soon found myself wanting an illu$tration gig.
But how to do illustration without burning out again? To answer this question, **Hundred Dollar Drawings** were born.

Hundred Dollar Drawings remove the worst parts of commercial illustration: contracts, submissions, revisions, and compromises that degrade the work until quality suffers and there's no fun to be had.

Here's how it works (adapted from my website, ninapaley.com):

HUNDRED DOLLAR DRAWINGS

I will draw your request for a mere $100. If you want the original drawing shipped to you, you MUST add $25. If you want a "making-of" video, that's another $100.

As this is an evolving experiment for me, I will be imposing ever-changing rules and restrictions. Current Rules:

1. No caricatures
2. Requests must be 2 words (or fewer)

If you have a special request, don't want to follow the restrictions, want a regular commercial contract, etc., you must contact me and offer way more money, because $100 is crazy cheap. I'm not saying I'll do it, but if I do, it will definitely cost more.

FAQ

Q: What if I don't like my drawing?

A: **Too bad, sorry.**

Q: Can you submit a sketch and let me comment for revisions?

A: **No. If you want revisions, commission another $100 drawing, and a third, fourth, etc. You can get 10 $100 drawings for less than my usual professional rate.**

Q: Can I use the drawing as a commercial logo for my business?

A: **Yes.**

Q: Can I use the drawing for advertising or other commercial purposes?

A: **Yes, anything you want.**

Q: Isn't that crazy cheap for commercial art?

A: **Yes. But some of these drawings are also non-commercial. It's all less stress for me, and I don't care what happens to the image after I draw it. (Actually I do care – the more it's used, the better.)**

Q: What about copyright?

A: **Like most of my work this is Free Culture. There's effectively no copyright to license or buy. You can do whatever you want with the art you commission, but it's non-exclusive. I will be posting it on my blog and social media.**

Q: What if I want exclusive rights?

A: **Then you'll have to pay more than $100 – same as most professional commercial art of this caliber. Shoot me an email to discuss.**

Q: What if Nina finds my drawing instructions abhorrent?

A: **I will refund your money and not do the drawing. Or I'll keep the money and willfully misinterpret your request. That might be more interesting.**

Q: Can you do a caricature if I send you a photo?

A: **No.**

This book contains many, but not all, of the Hundred Dollar Drawings to date, along with a few more-than-$100 "special requests". These drawings aren't perfect; nothing ever is. But additional negotiations, notes, and revisions wouldn't have improved them. For me, the greatest success of this project is I still enjoy drawing as much as I did when I started. Would a conventional illustration gig have yielded that outcome? I don't want to rule it out, but I've never before done so many drawings with so little anguish. I look forward to drawing more.

I would like to thank everyone who requested a drawing (or multiple drawings) and put their literal money where their figurative mouths are. In addition to supporting me materially, you have challenged me, and given me reasons to draw when I was too lazy to think of my own.

—Nina Paley
21 December 2016
Urbana IL

These drawings are printed on one side only, so you can tear them out and frame them, as befits an Adult Coloring Book.

The two-words-or-less prompts that inspired each drawing are printed on the backs (more-than-two-word special requests are designated as such).

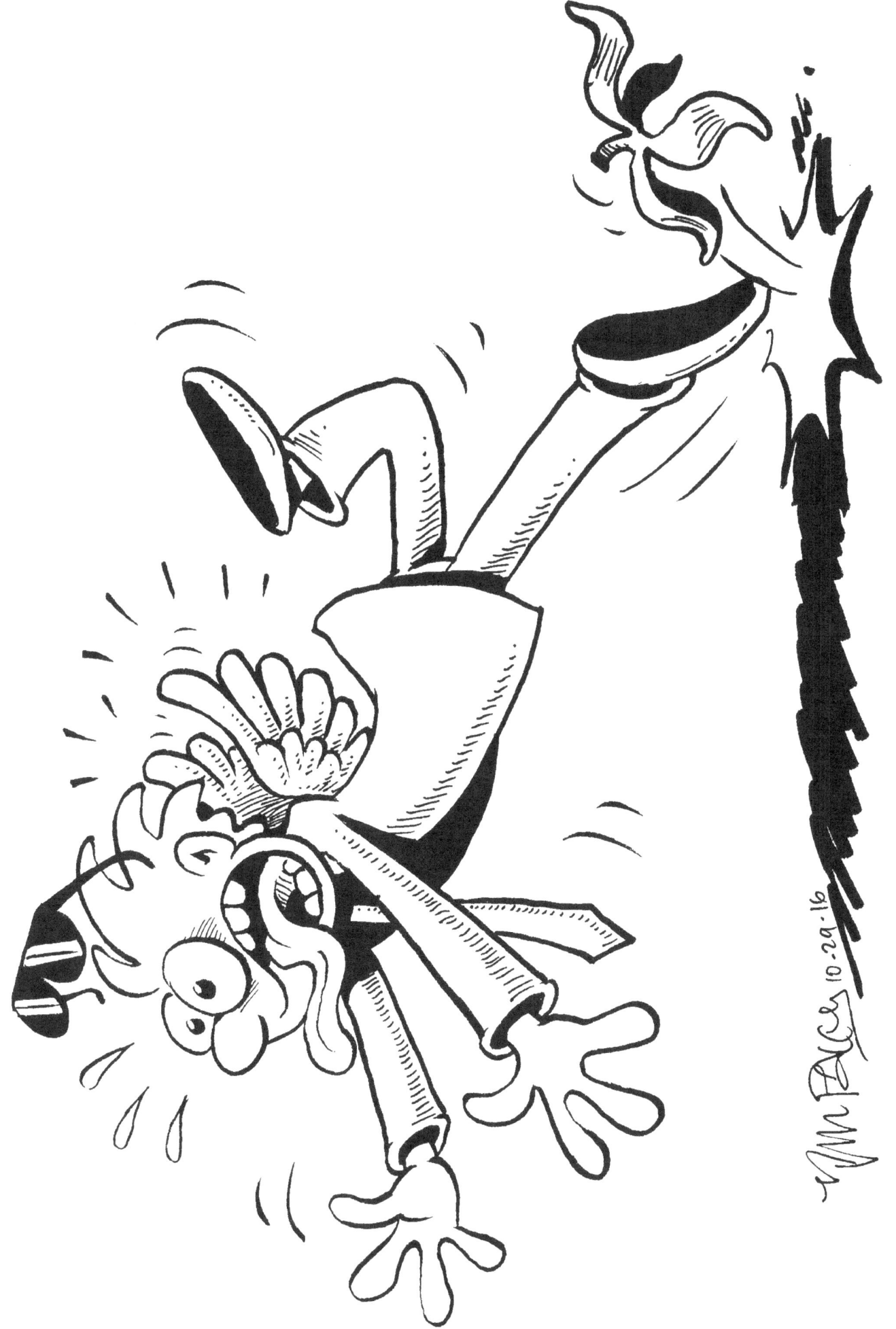

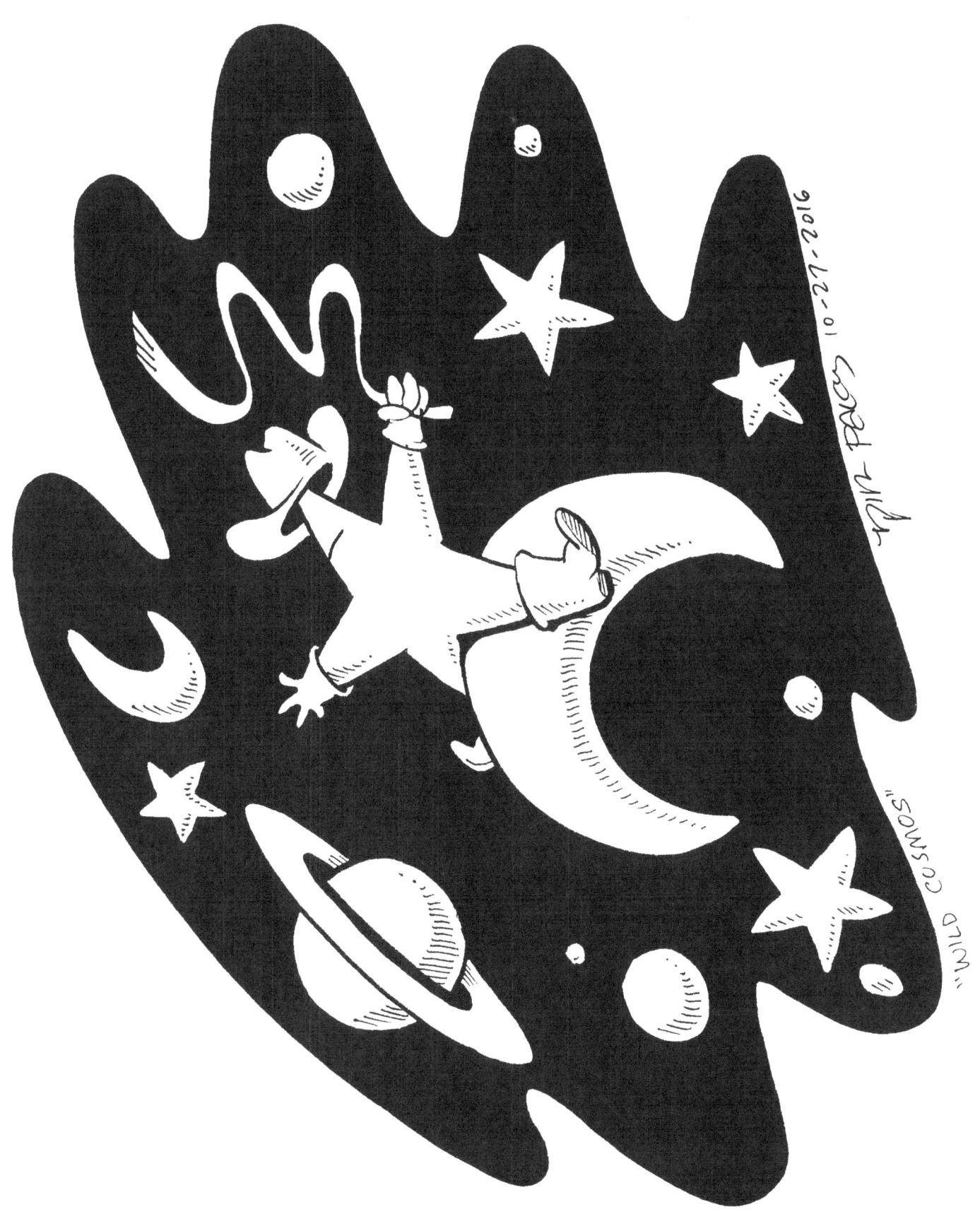

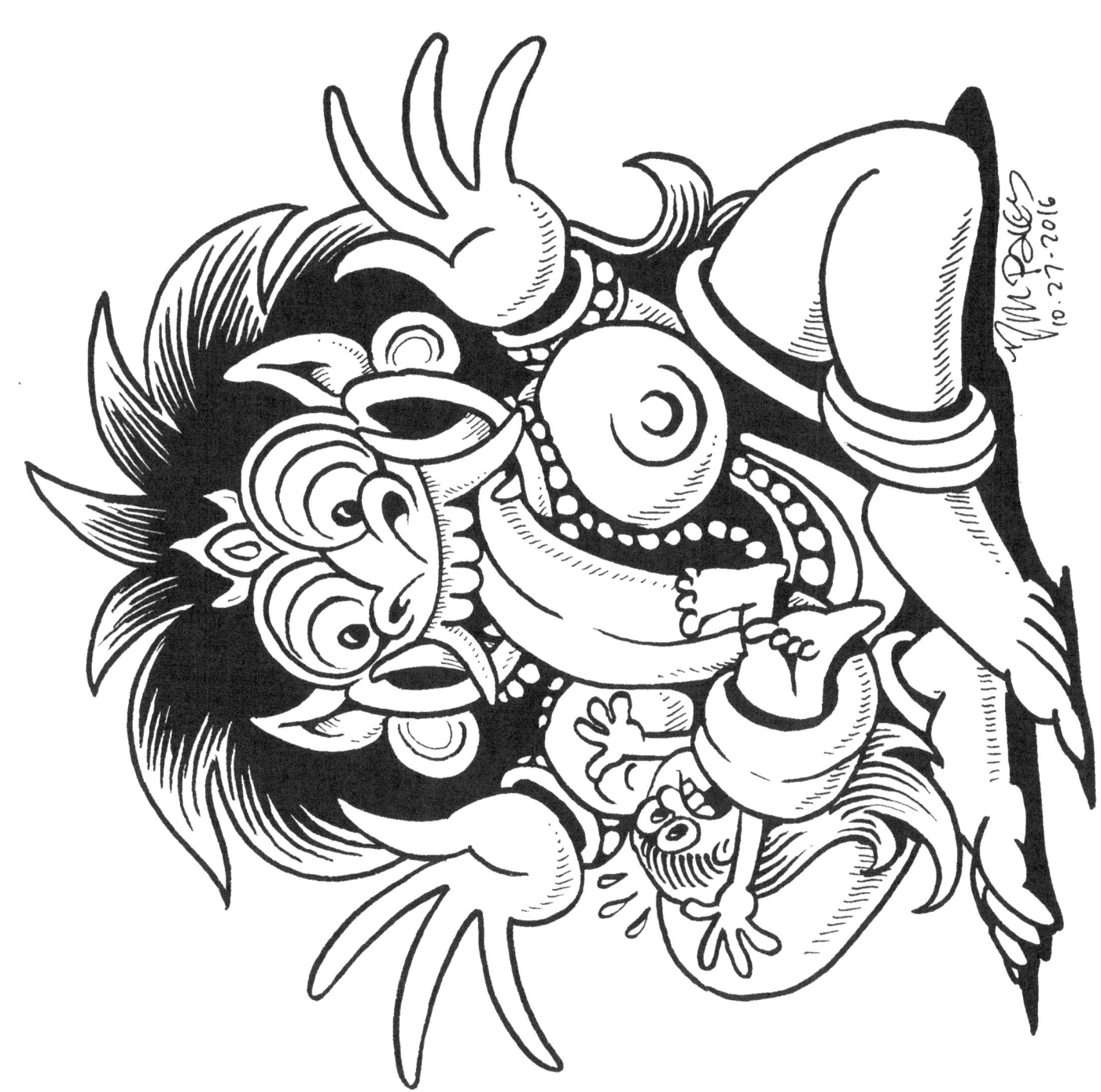

"Hindu Bali" (Rangda)

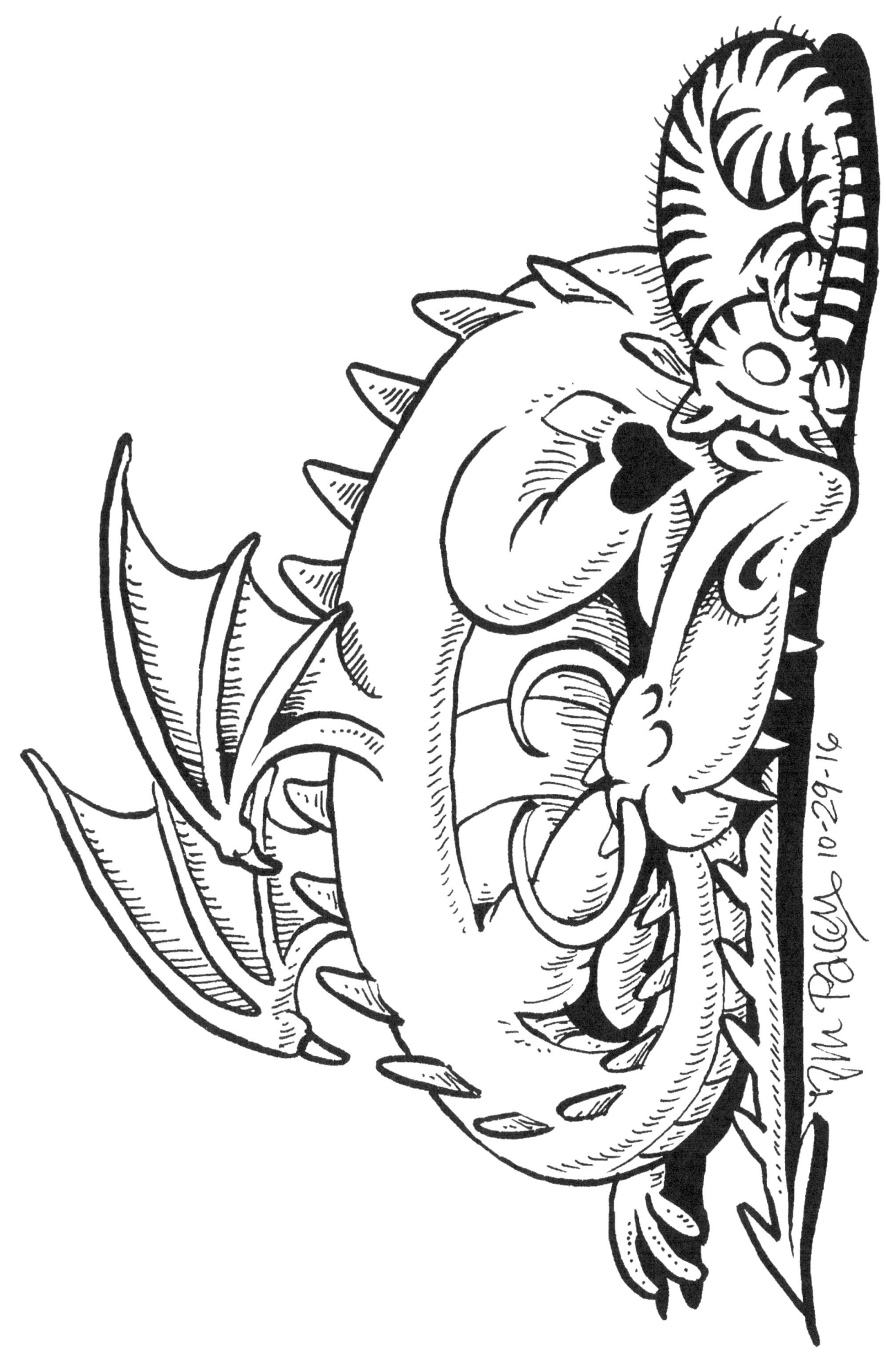

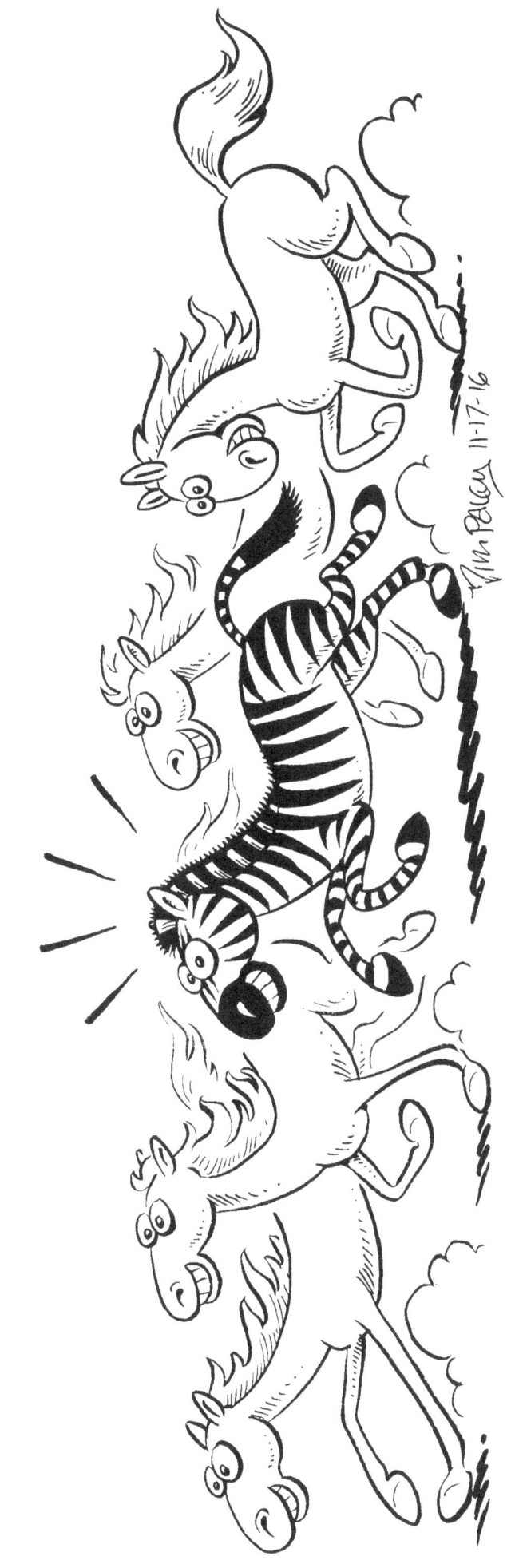

Special Request: "A Zebra running in a herd of horses"
(for Carcinoid and Neuroendocrine Cancer Awareness)

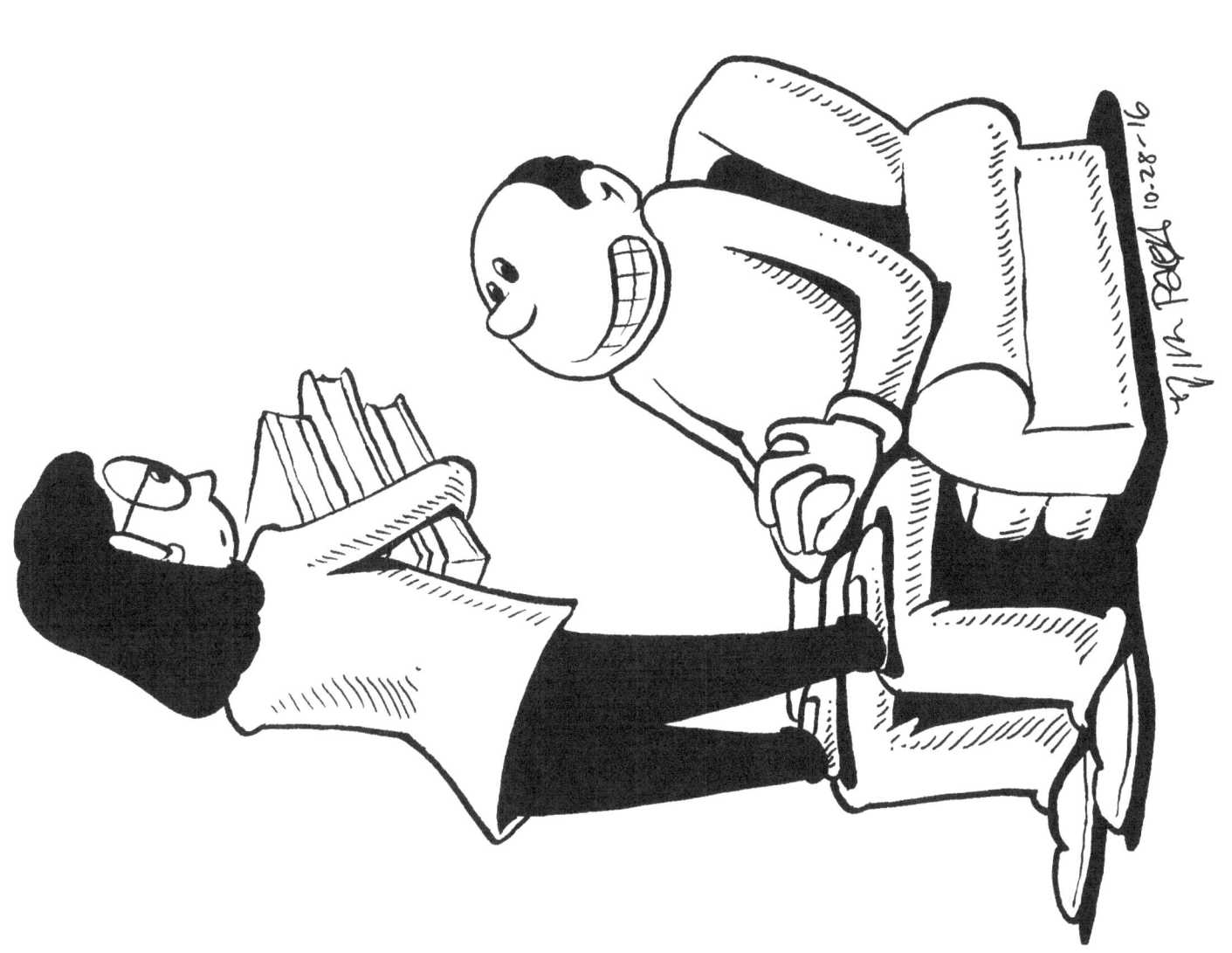

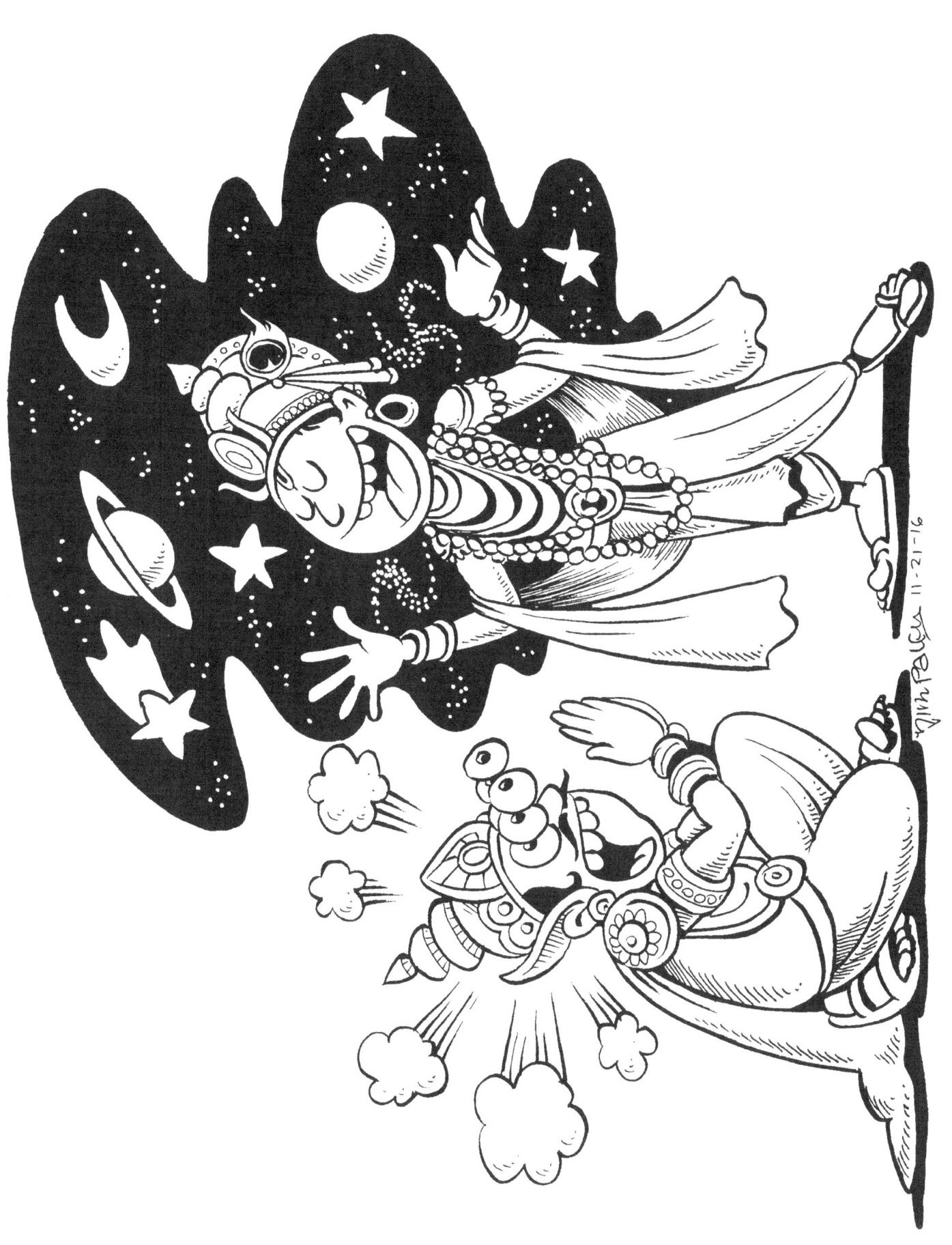

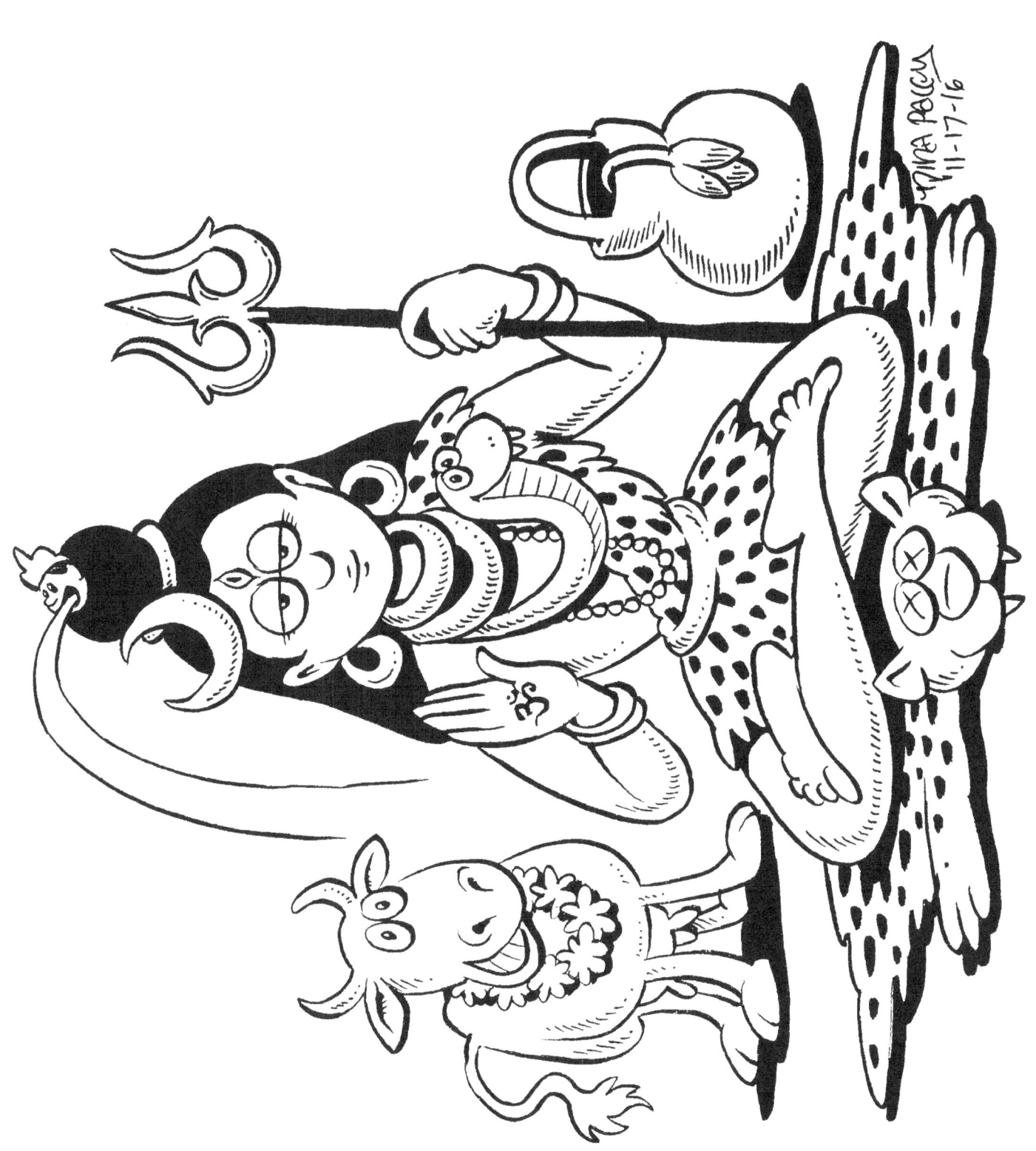

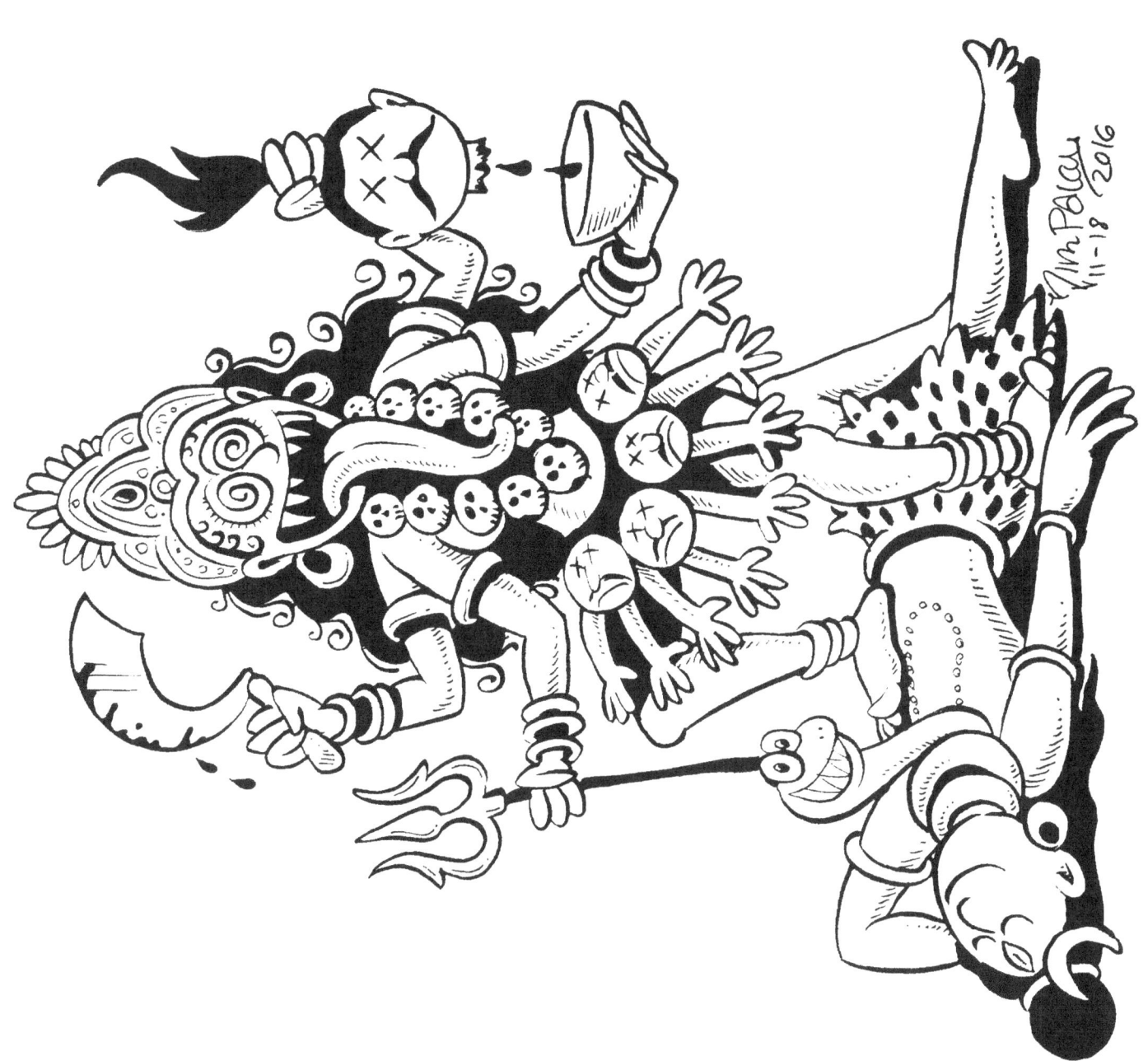

"Kali"

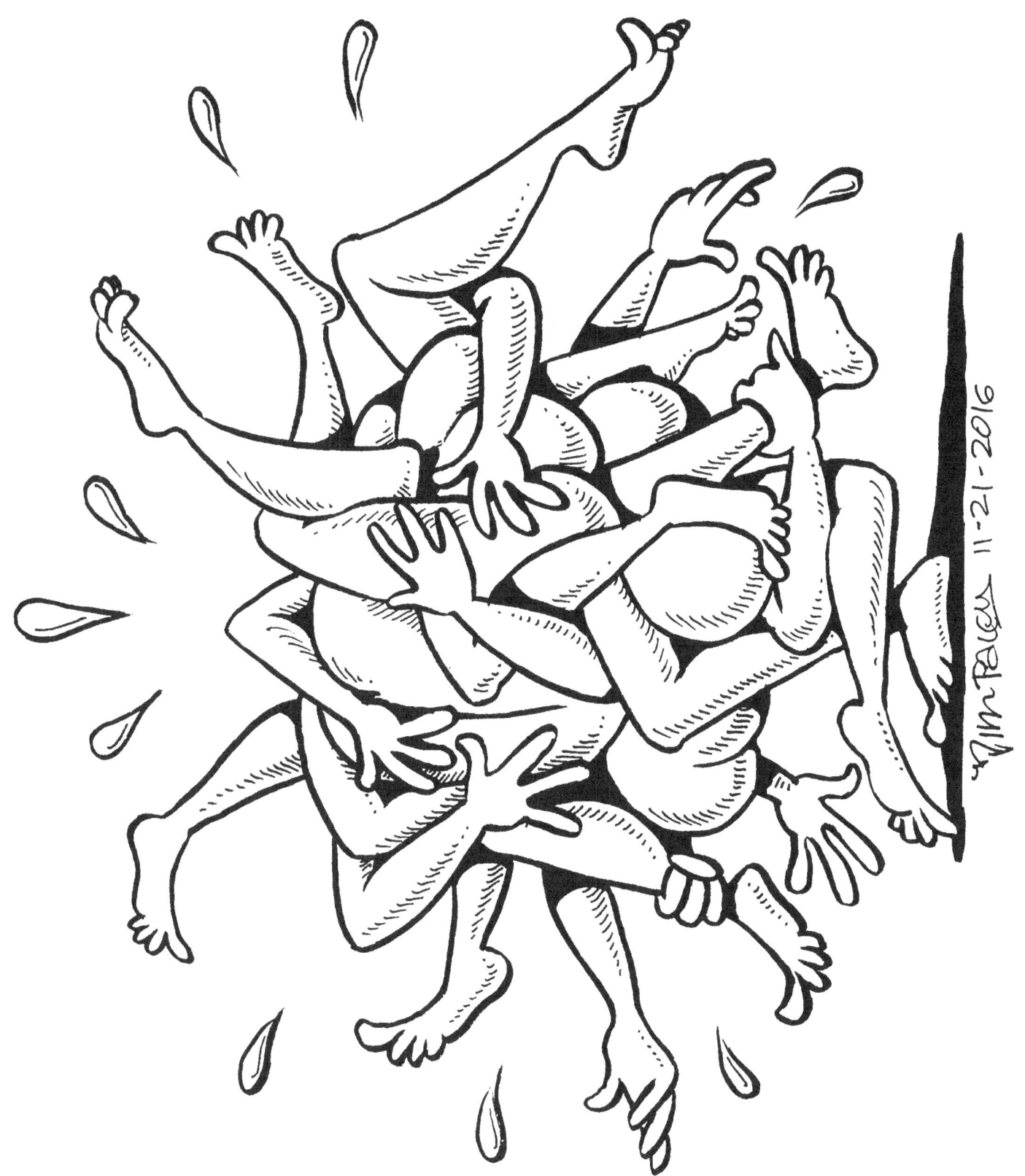

"Kama Sutra"

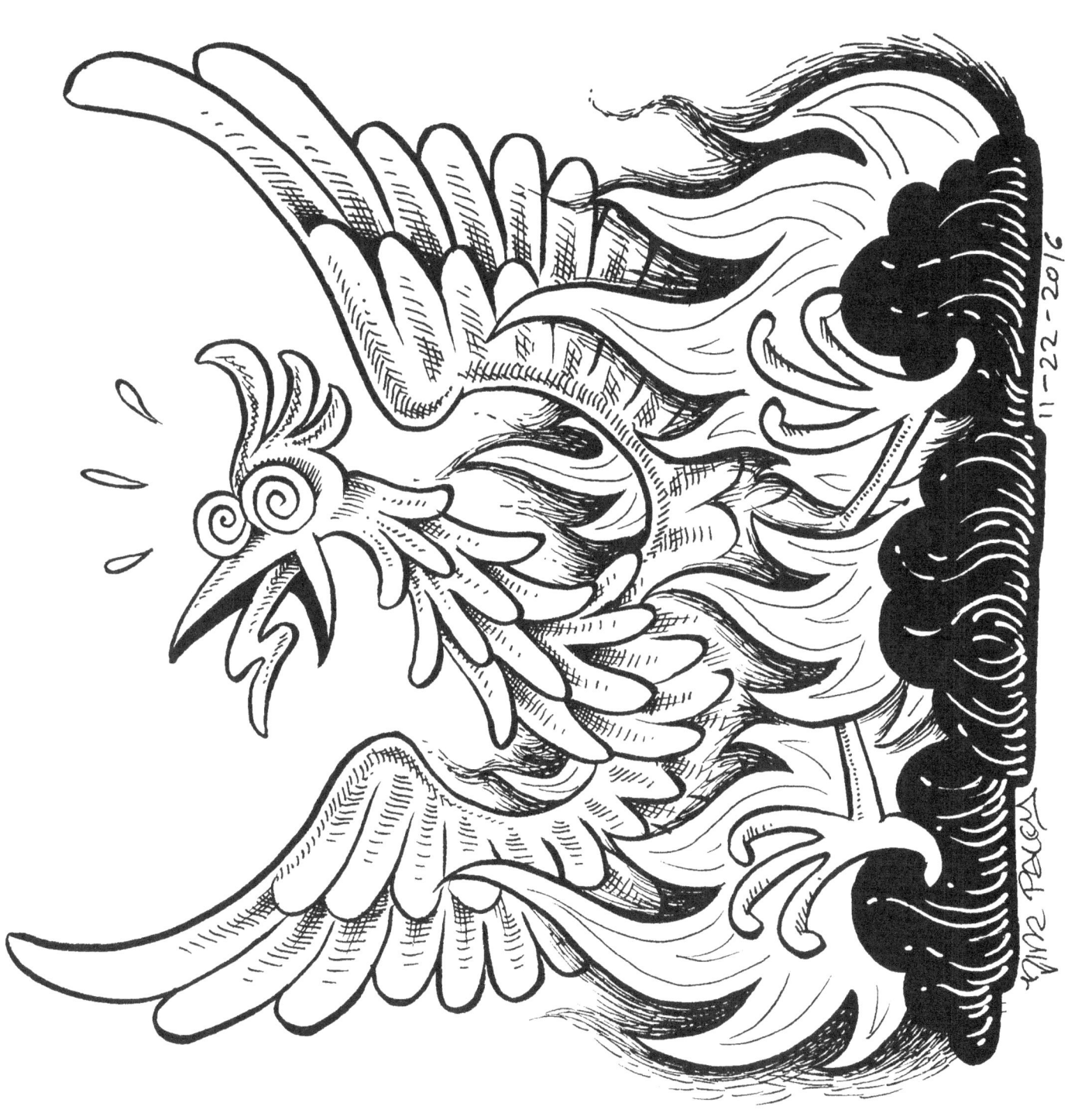

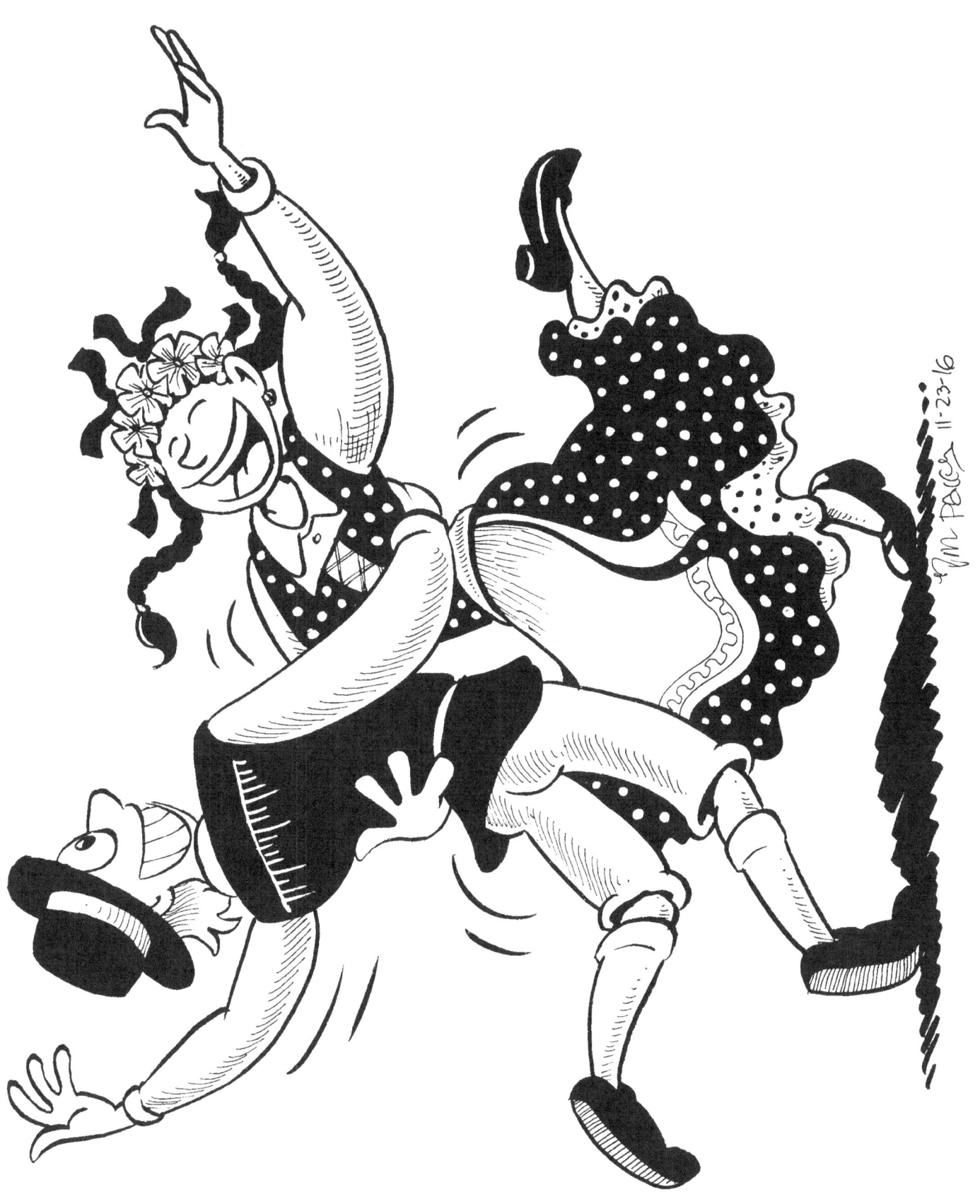

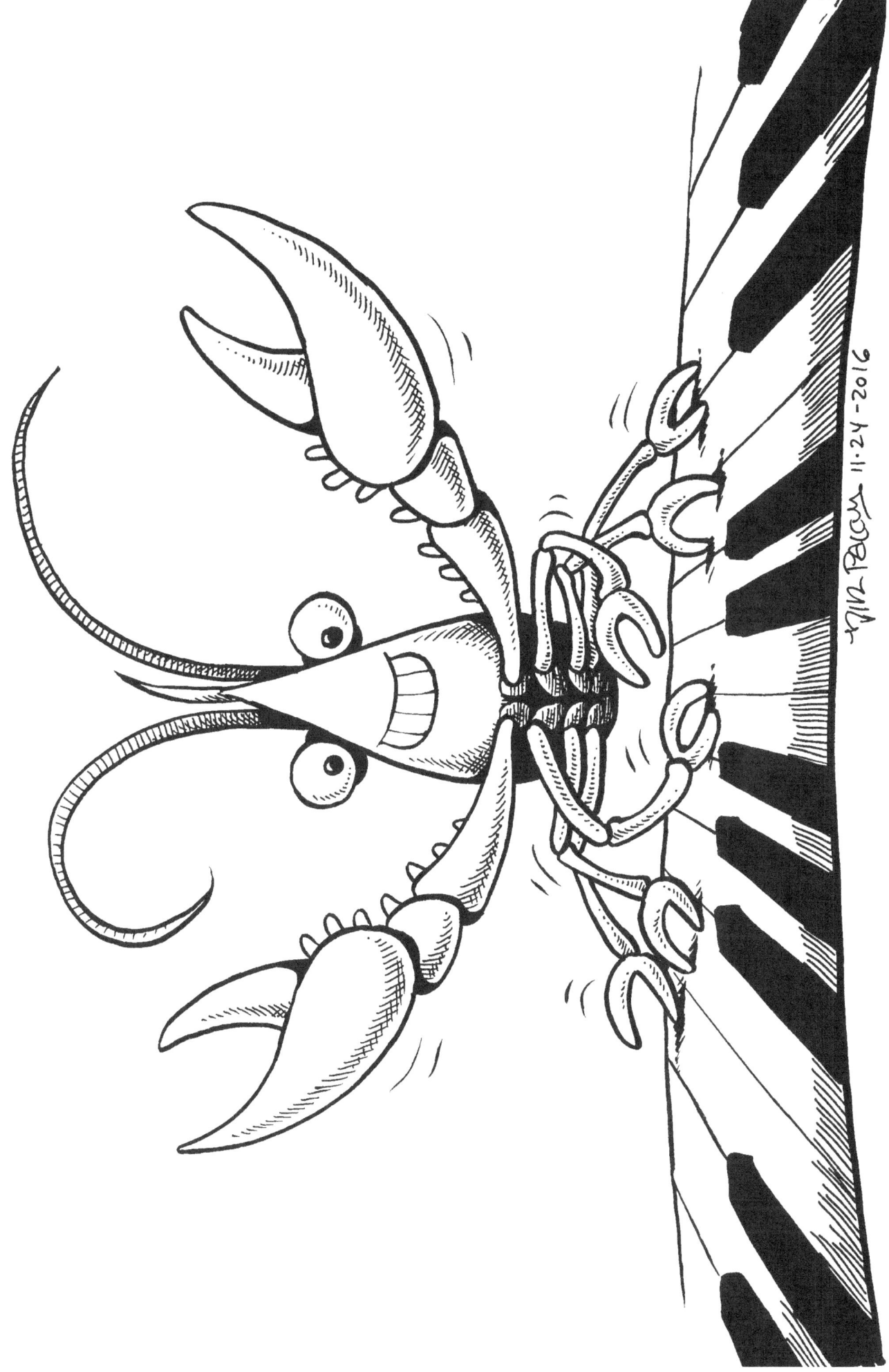

"Crawdad Piano"

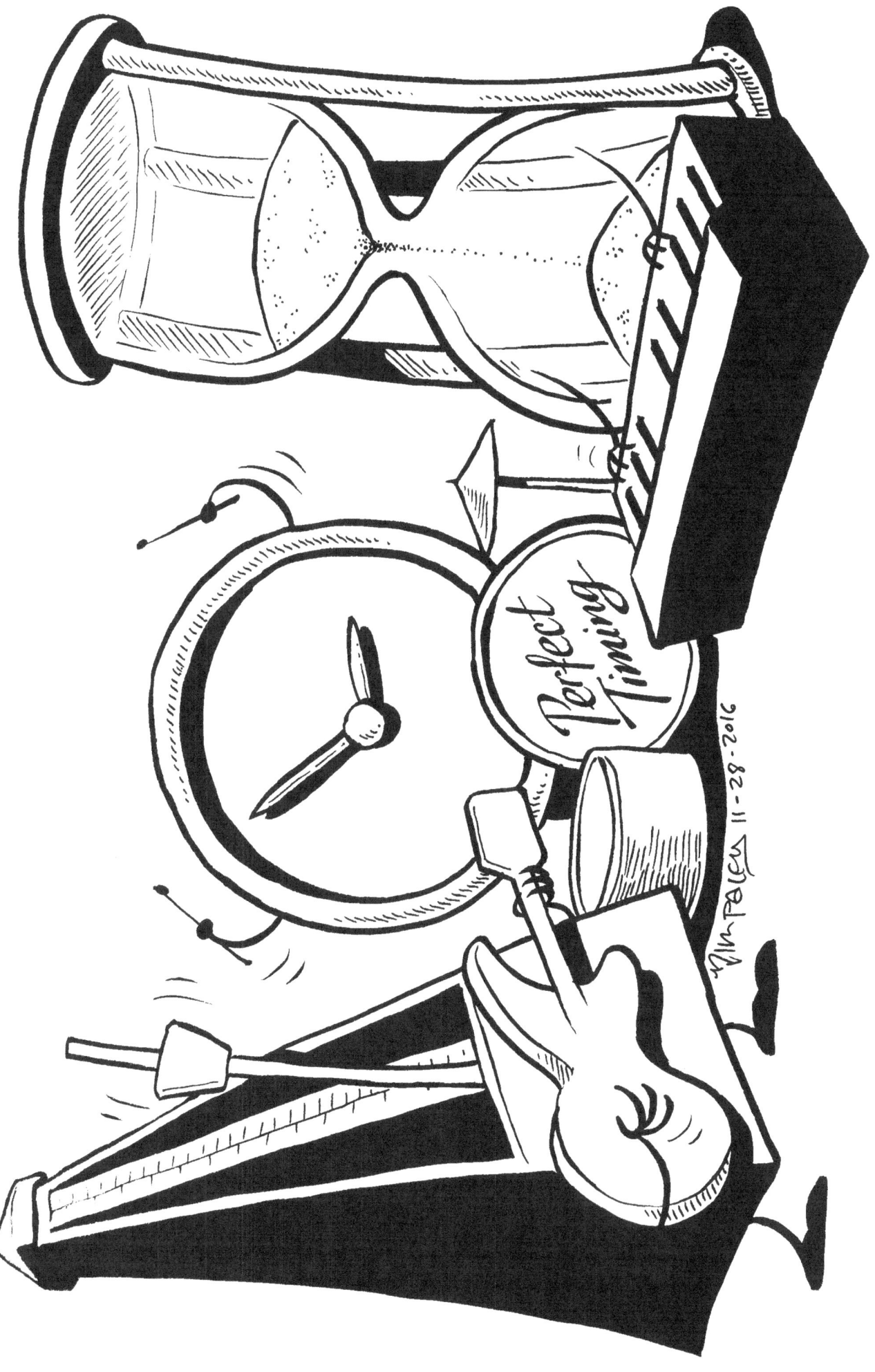

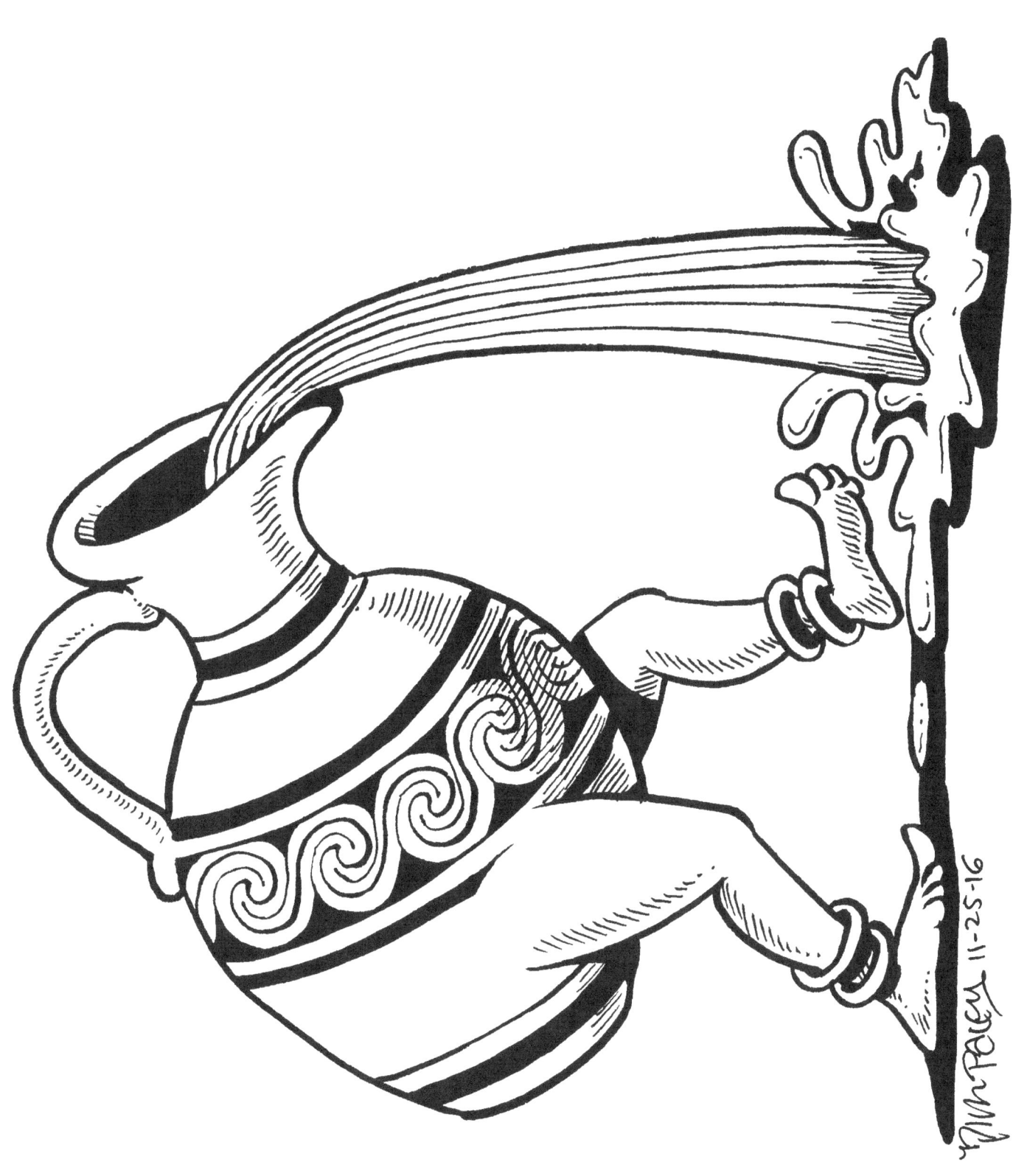

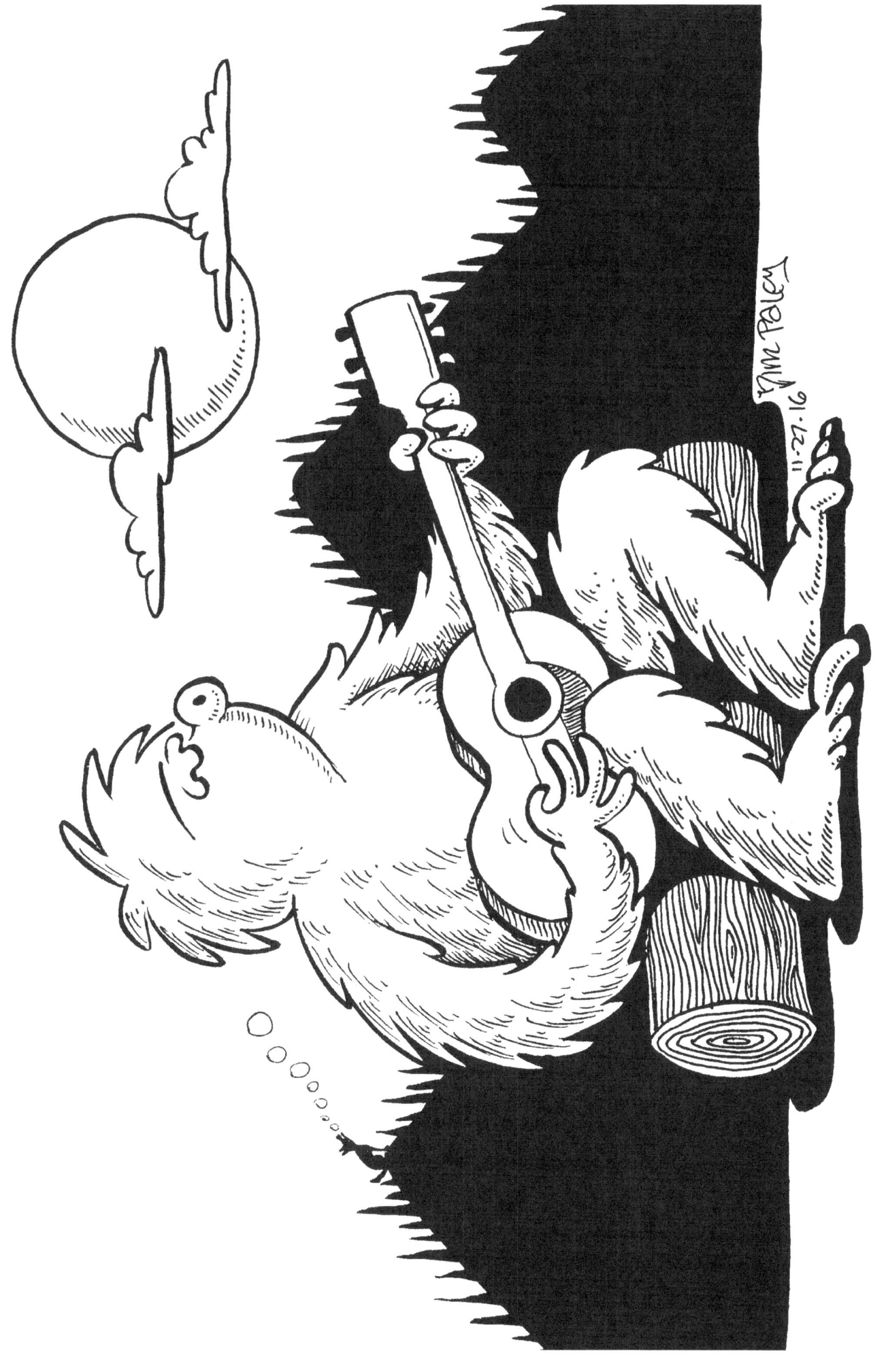

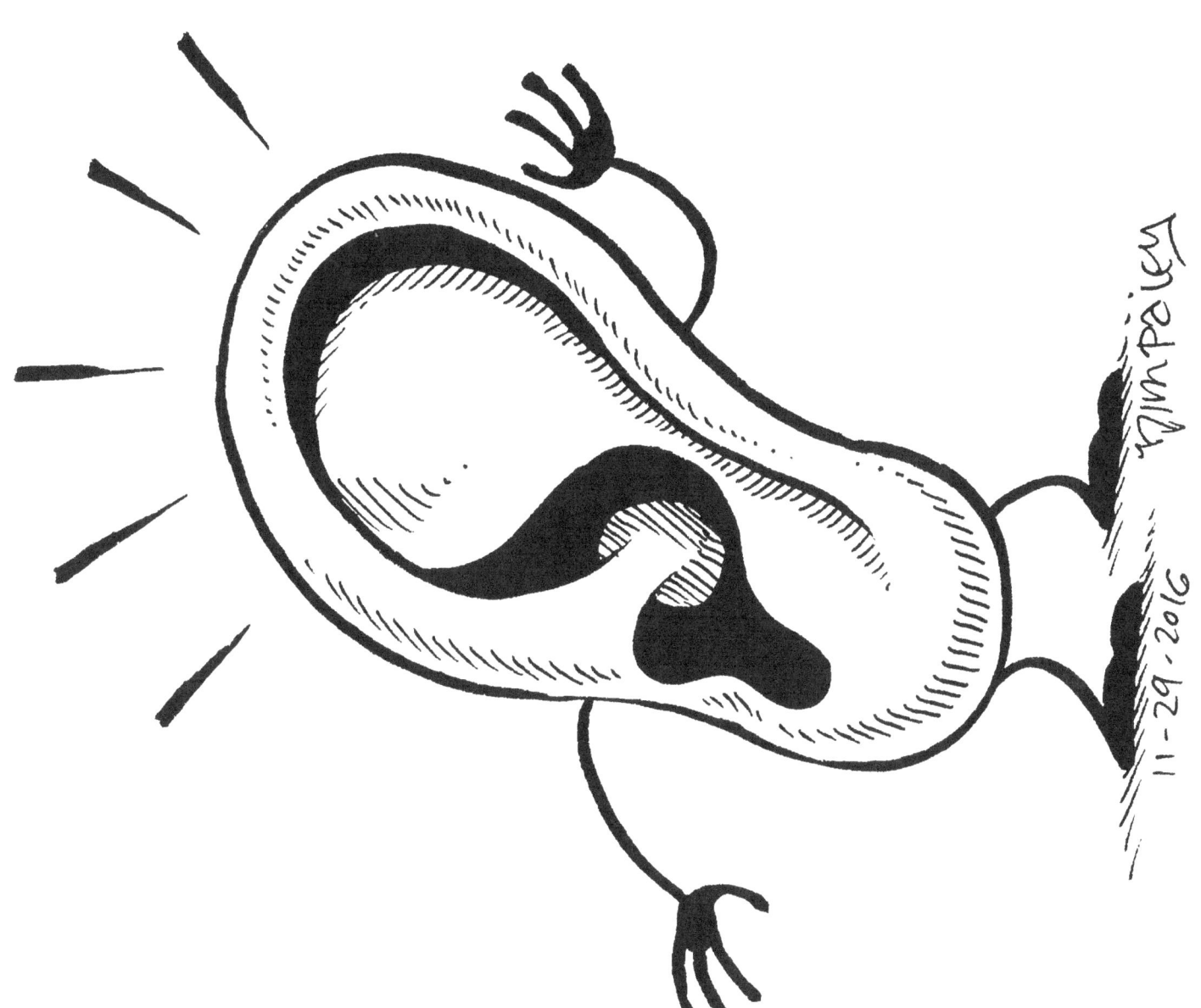

11-29-2016

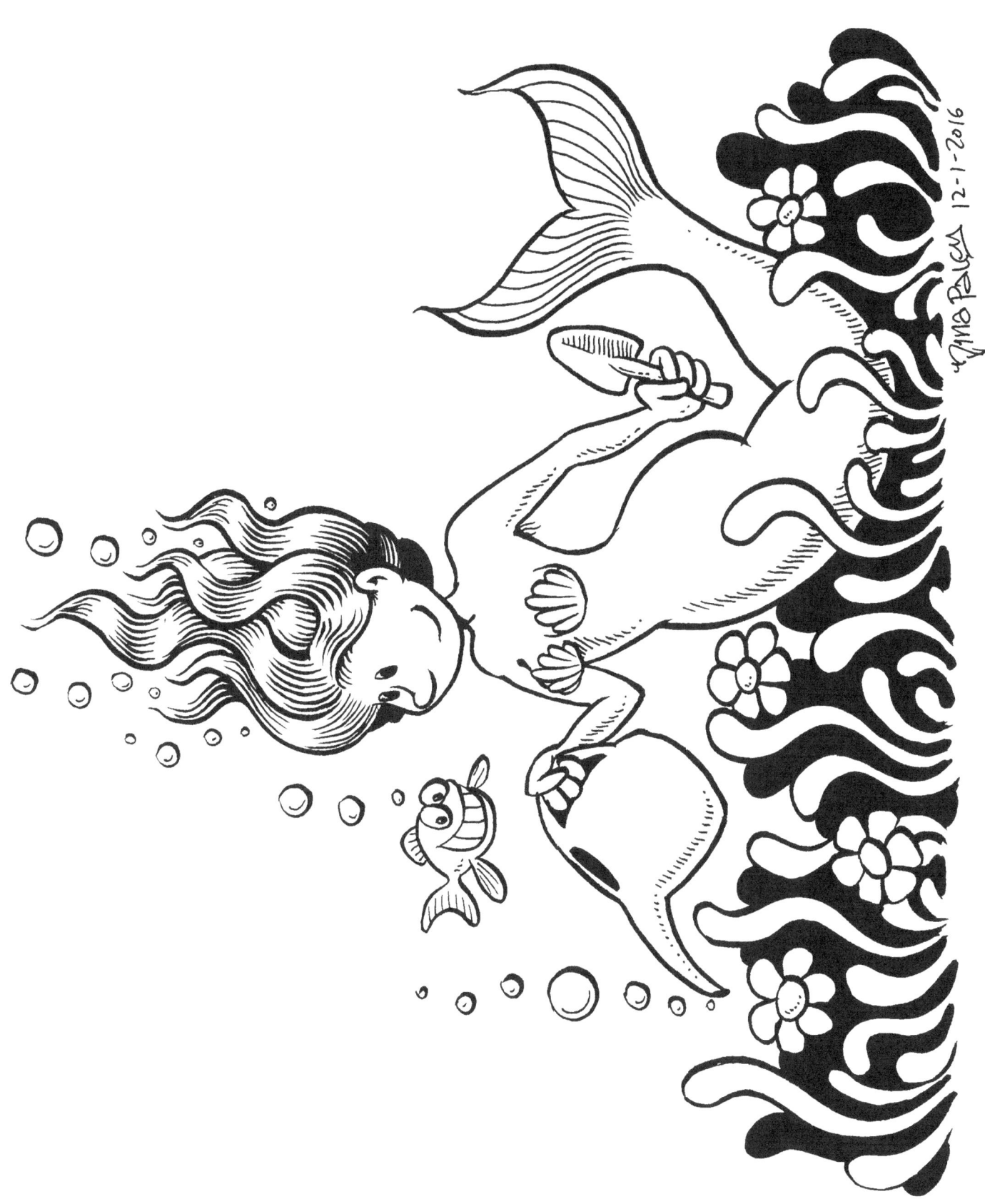

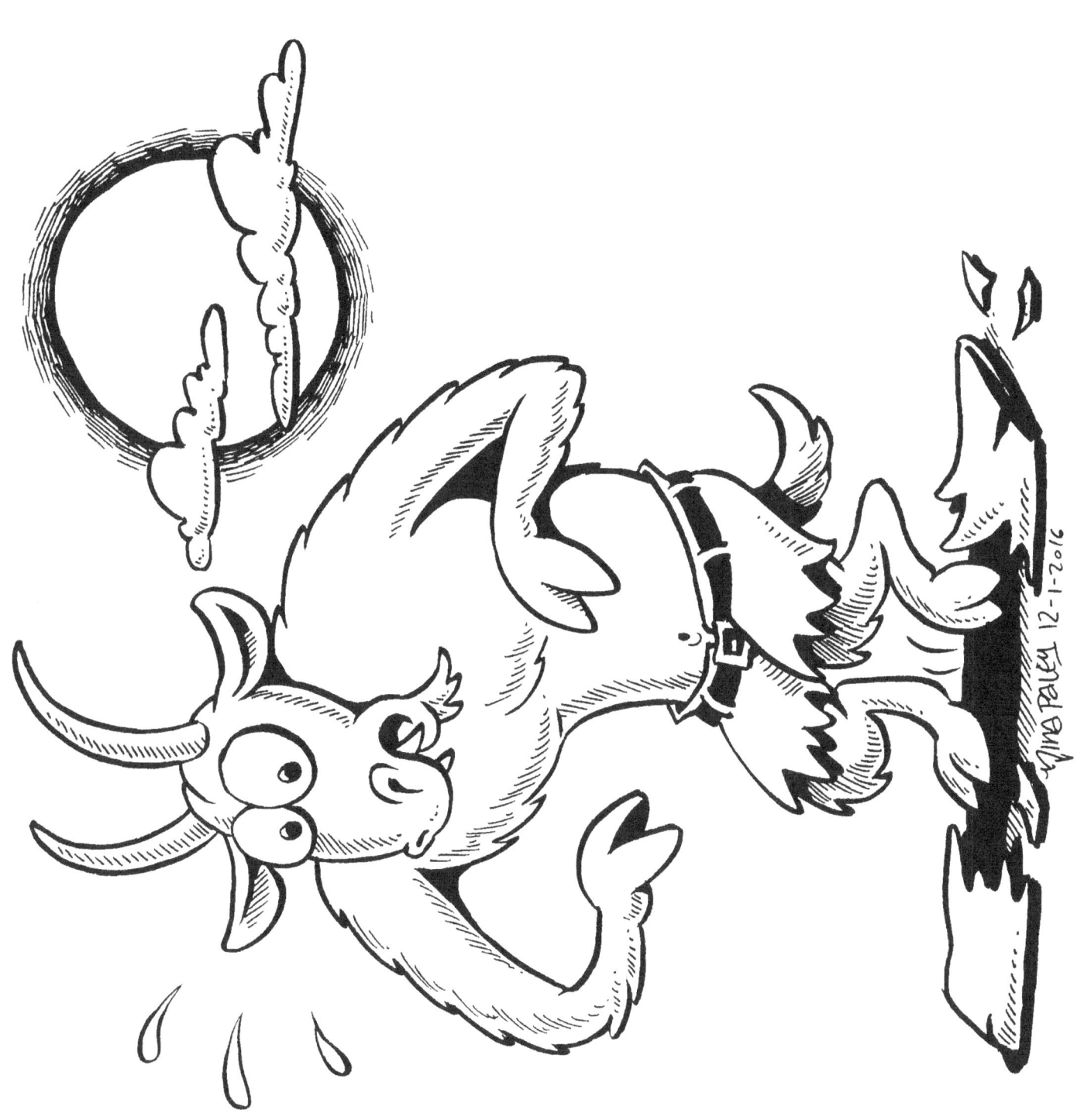

"Weregoat"

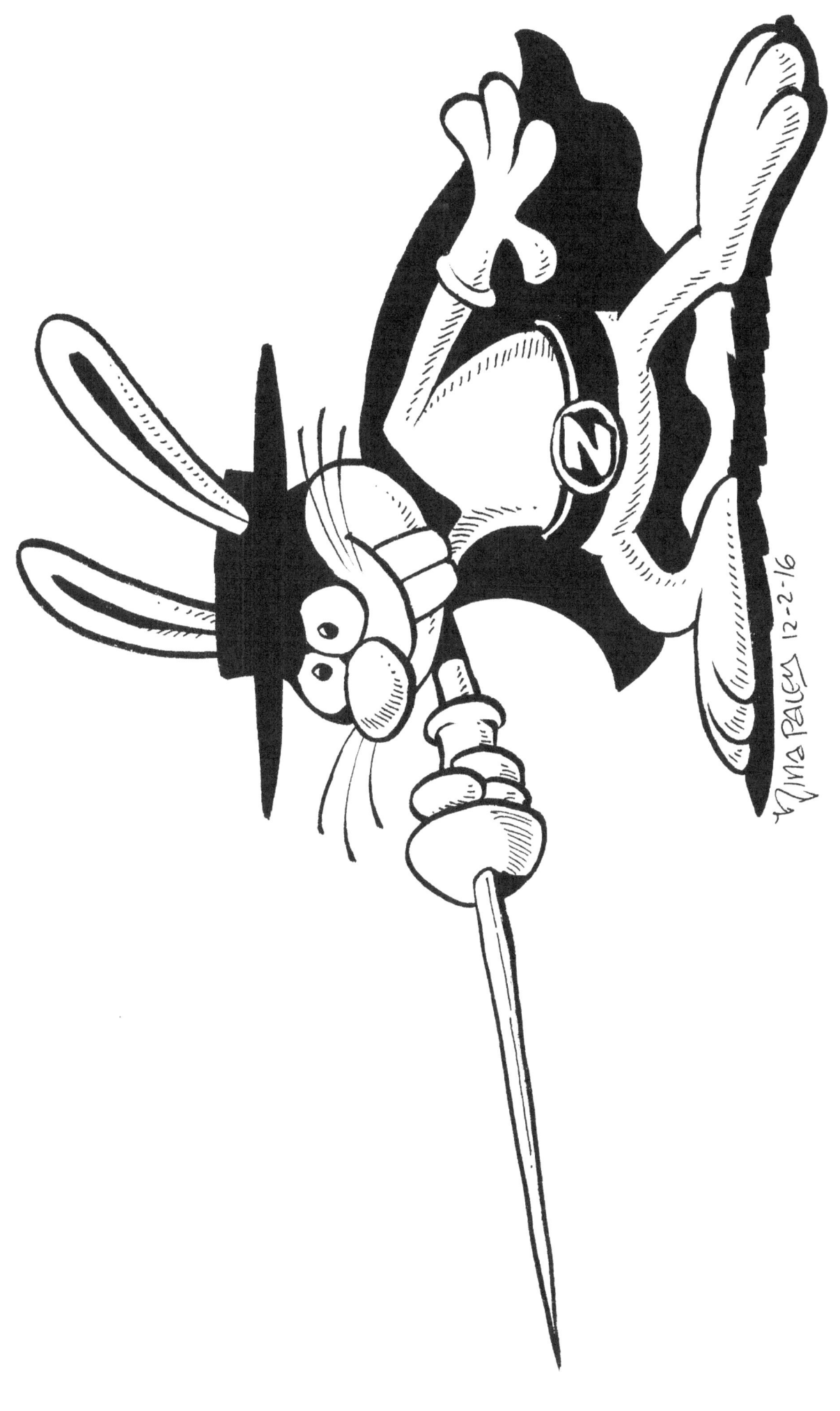

Jim Palom 11·25-2016

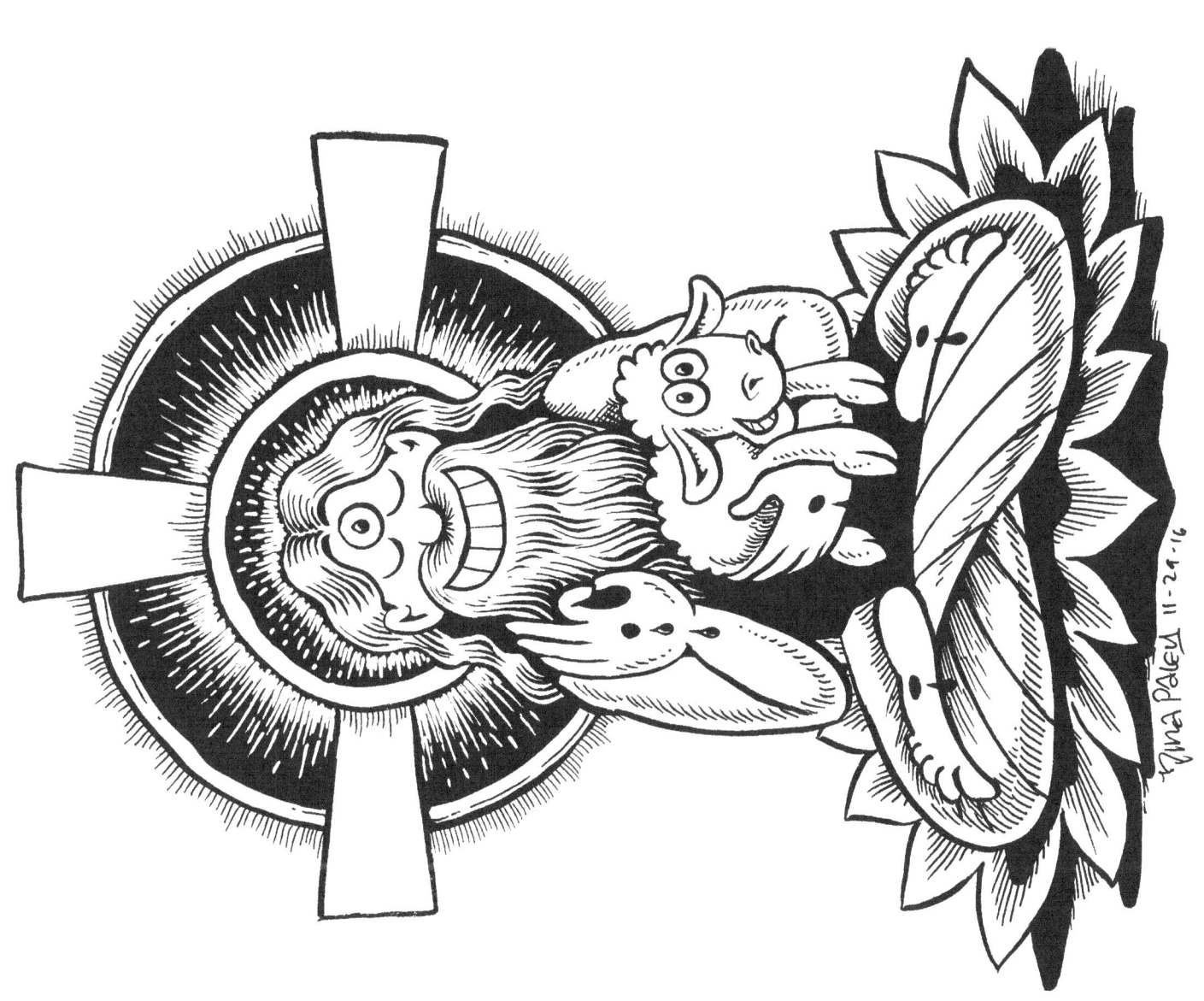

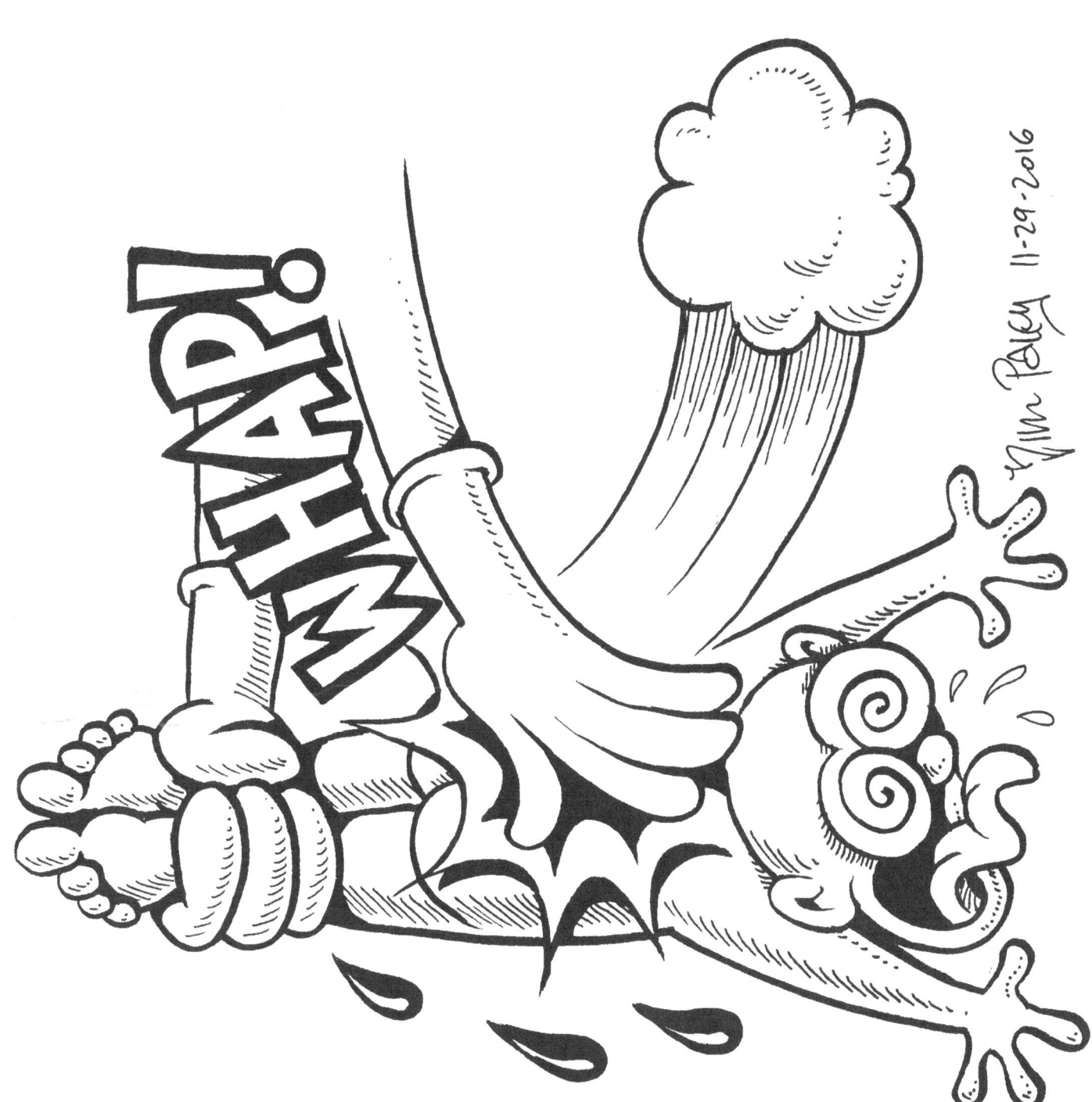

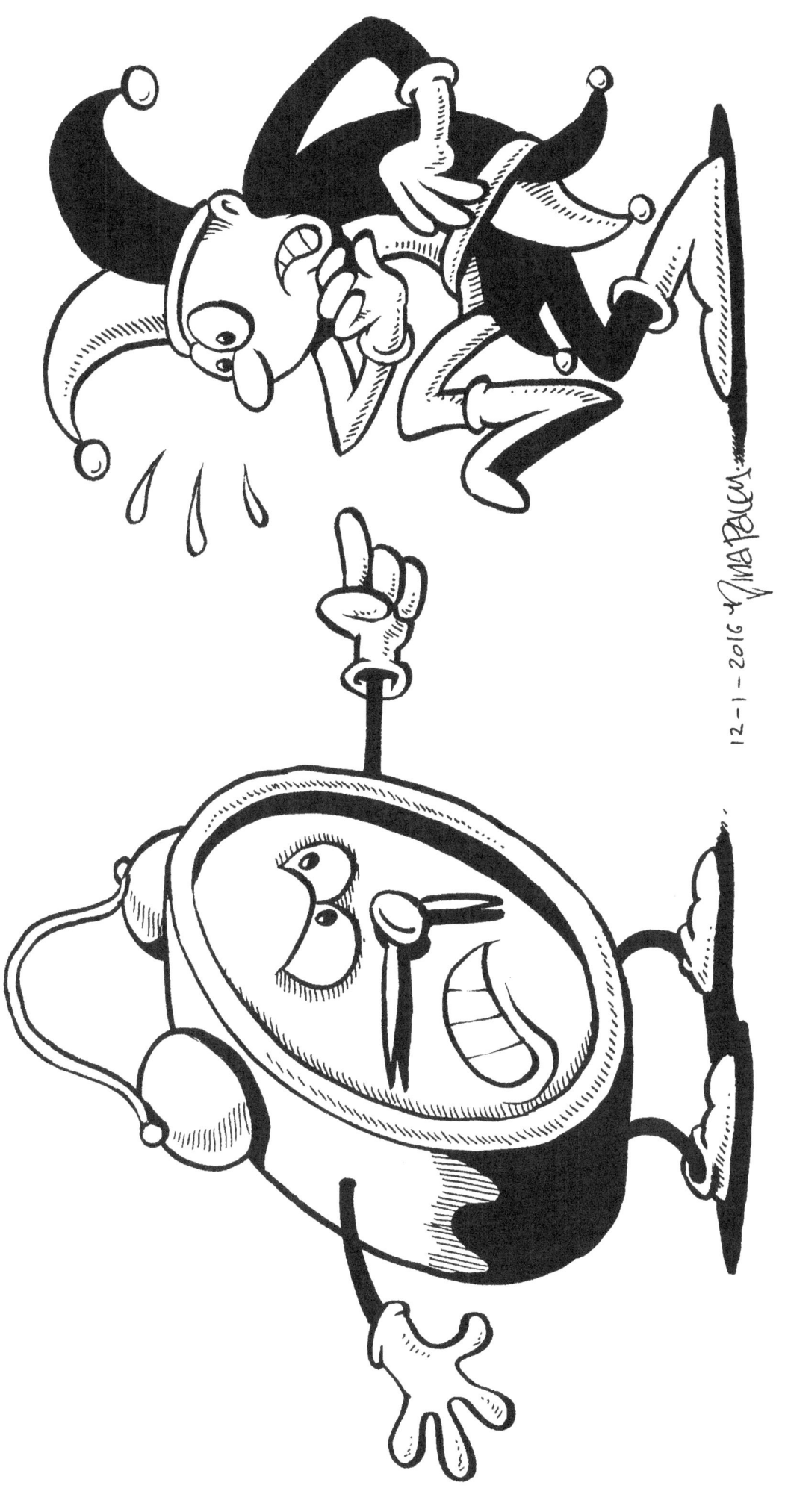

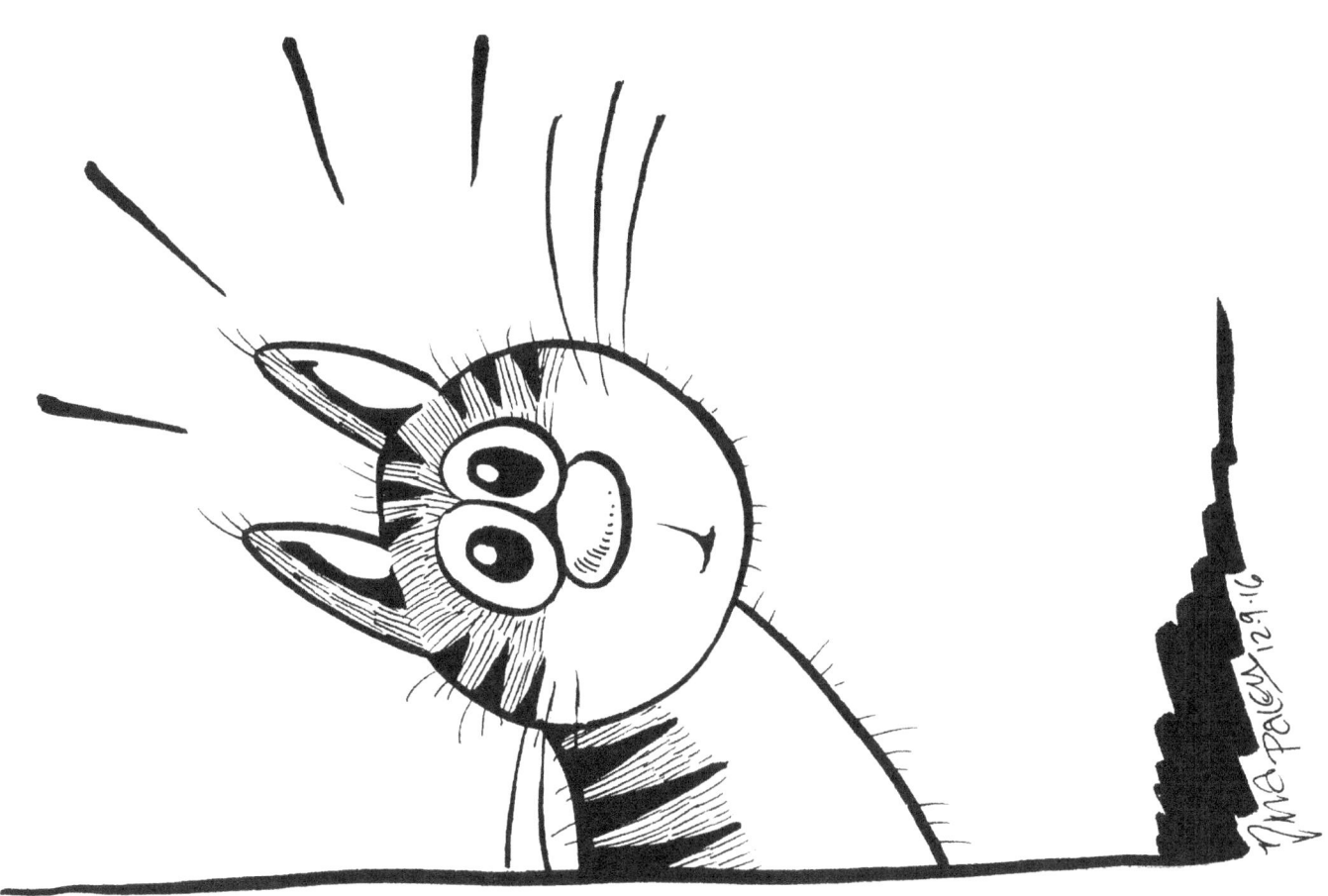

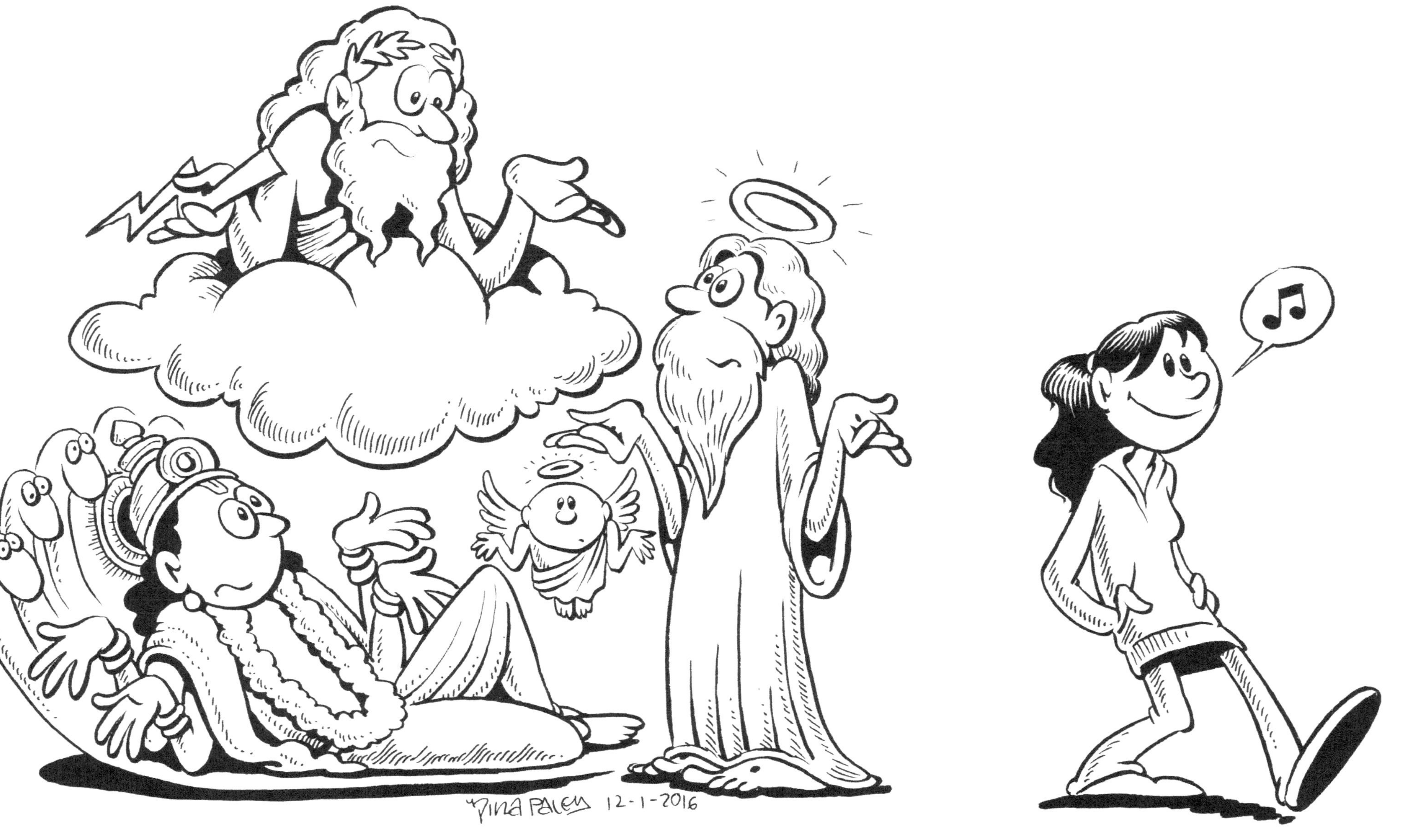

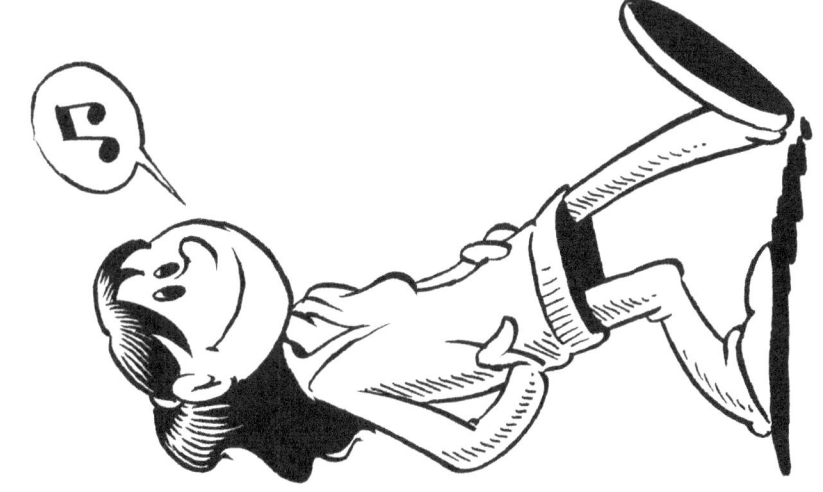

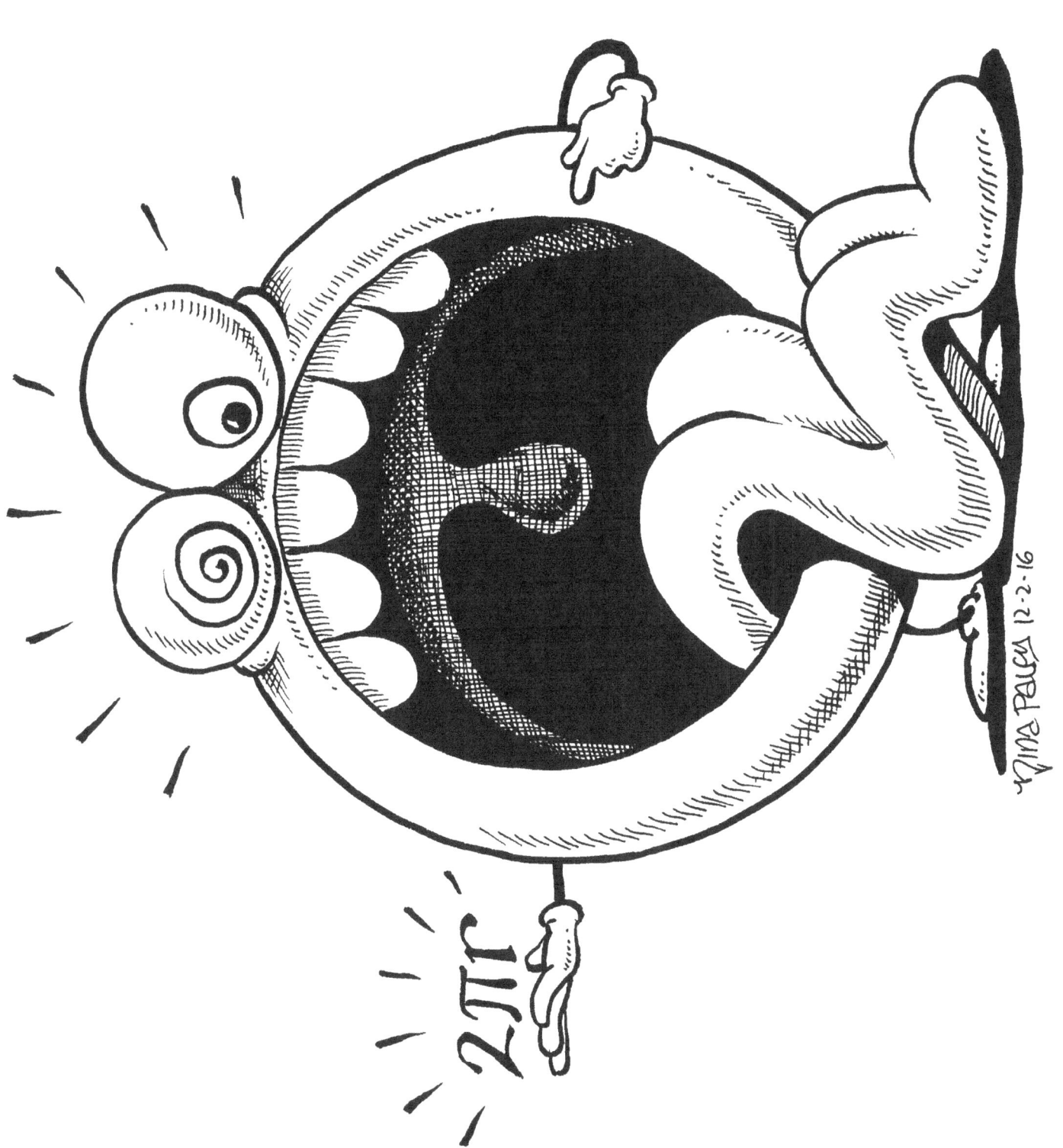

$2\pi r$

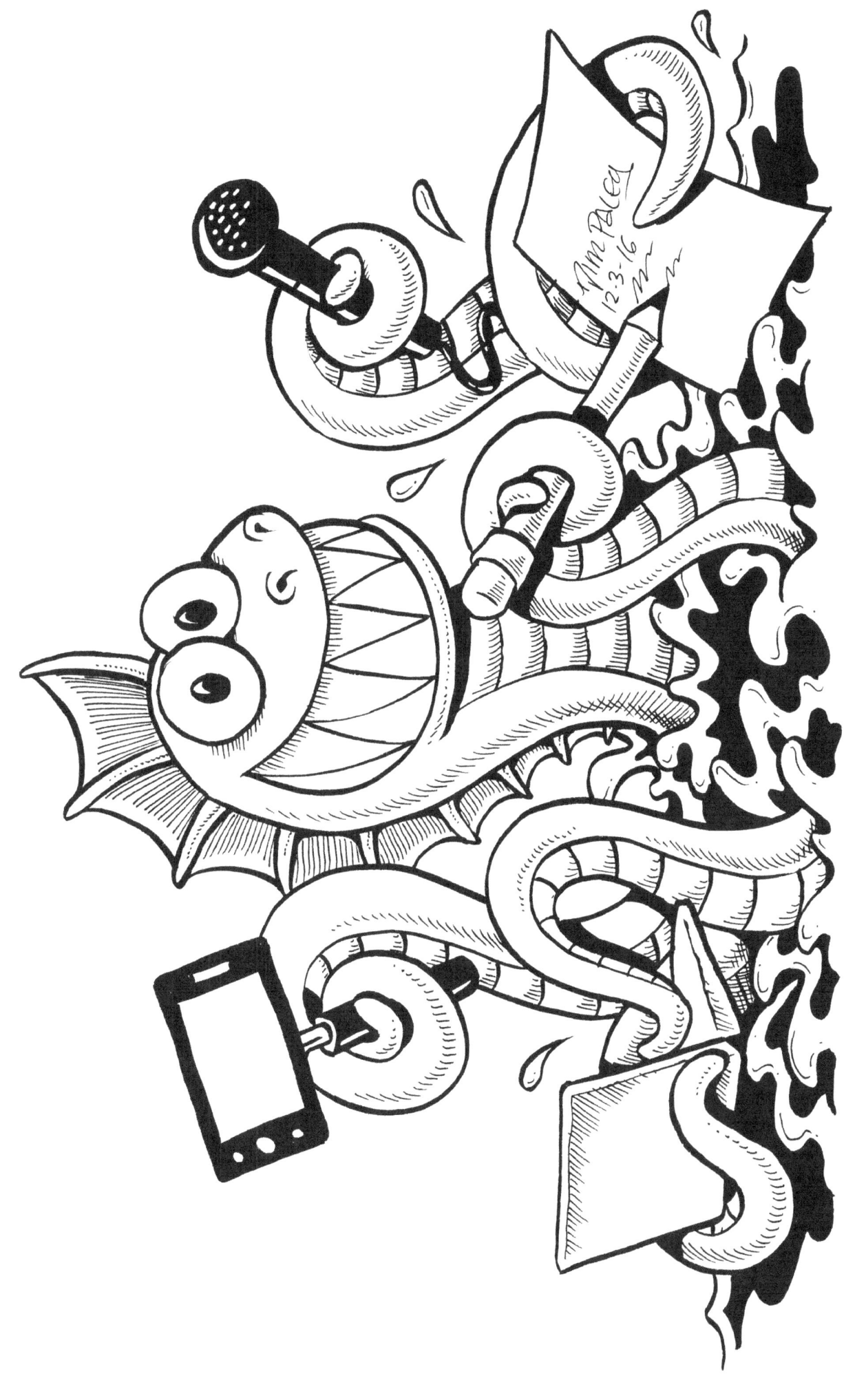

"Content Kraken"

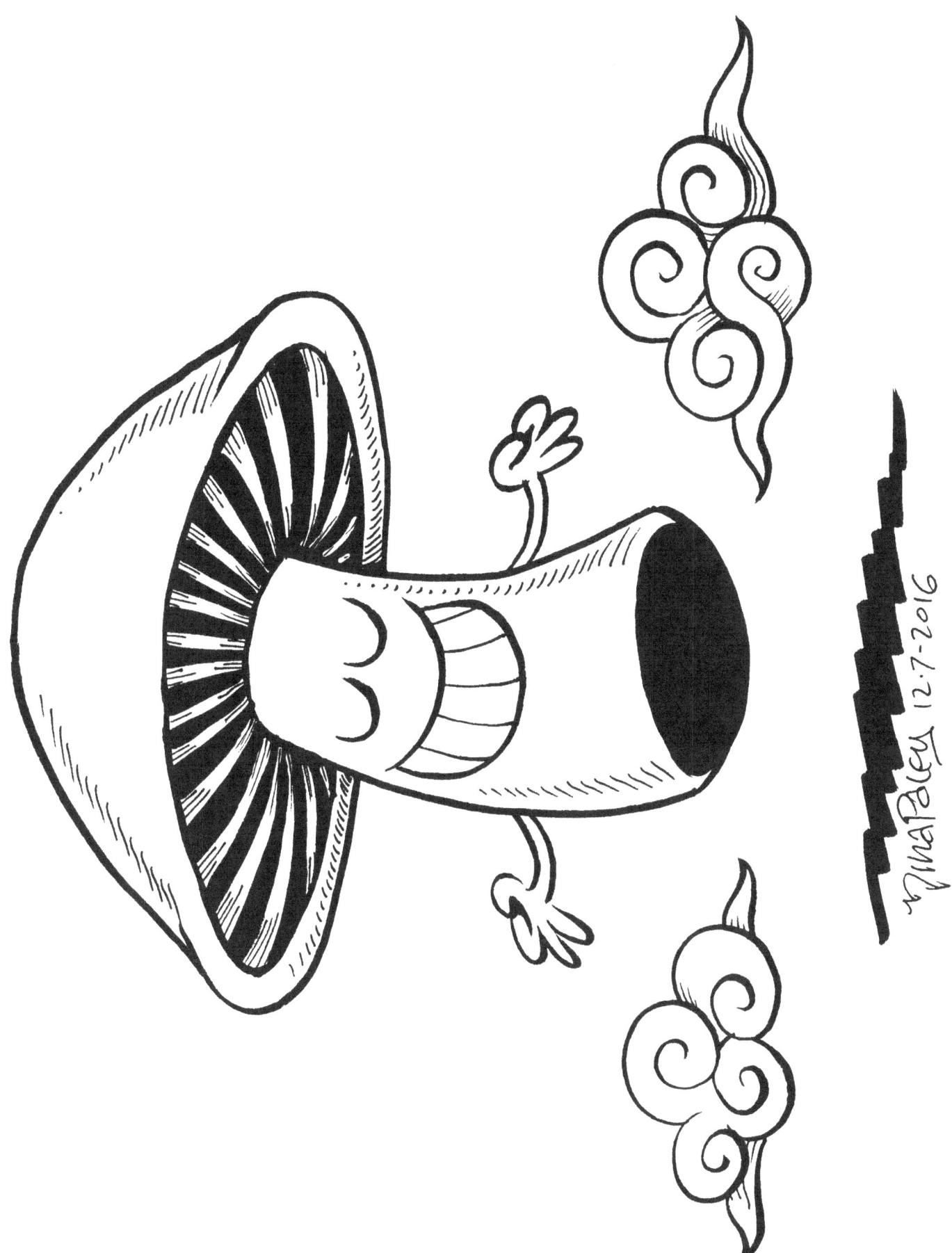

Pina Paley 12-7-2016

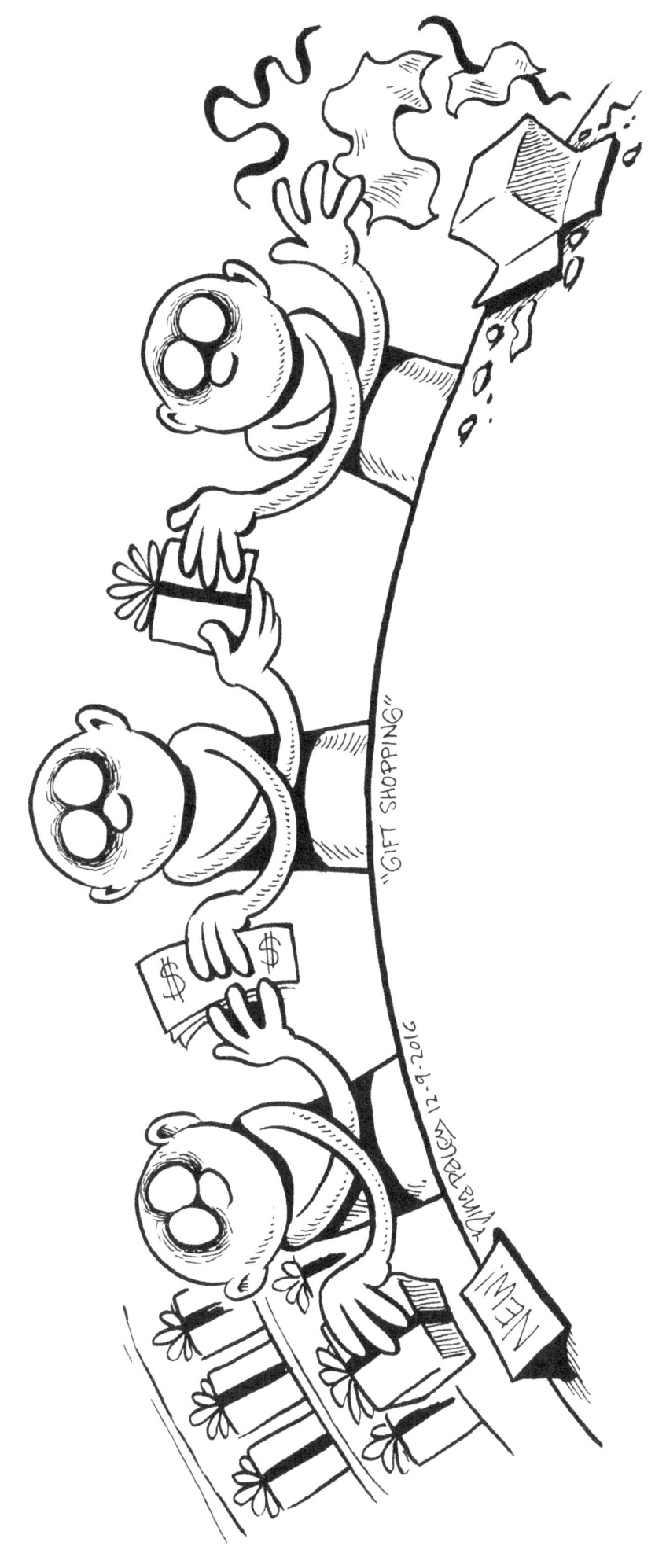

"GIFT SHOPPING"

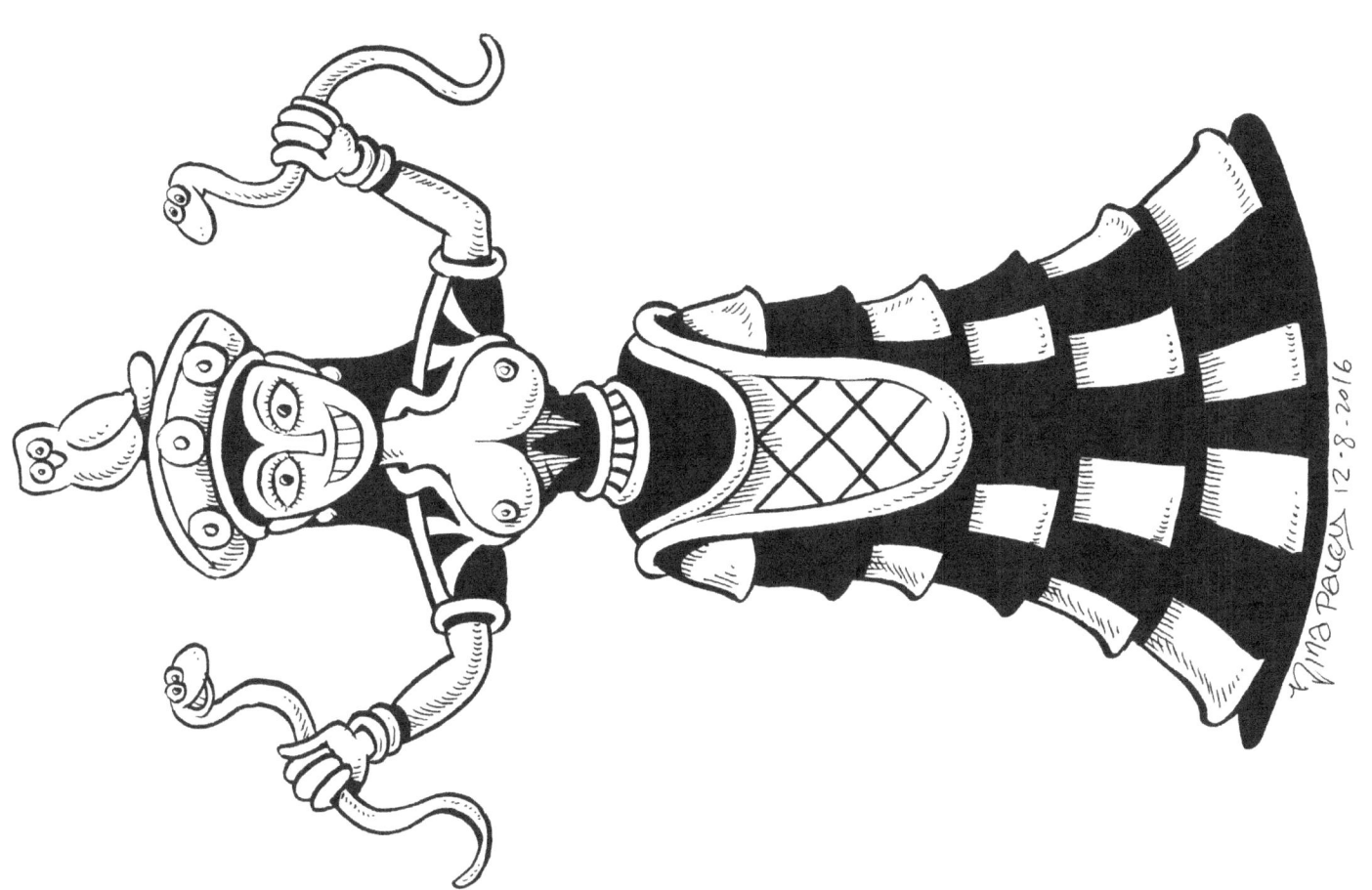

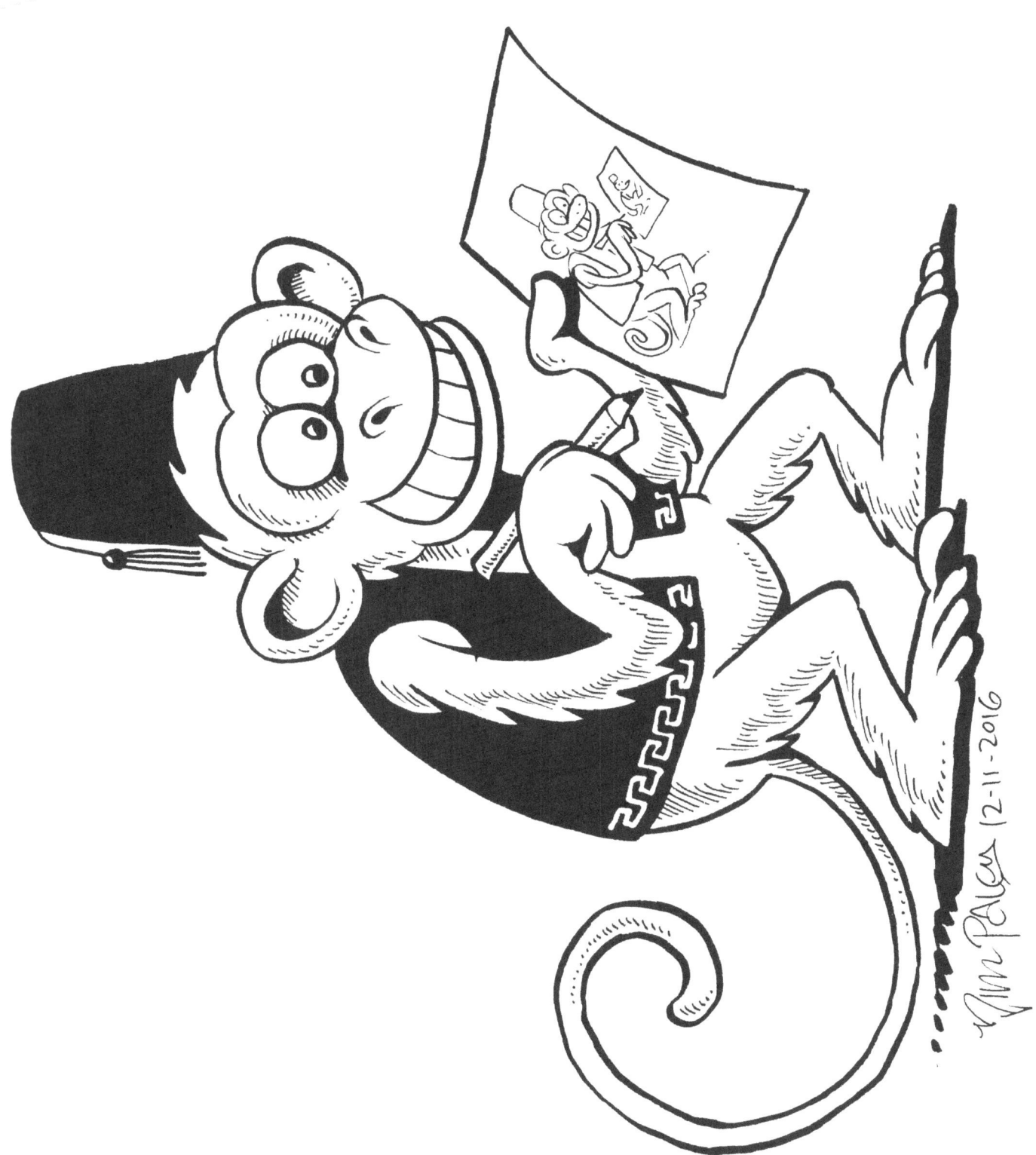

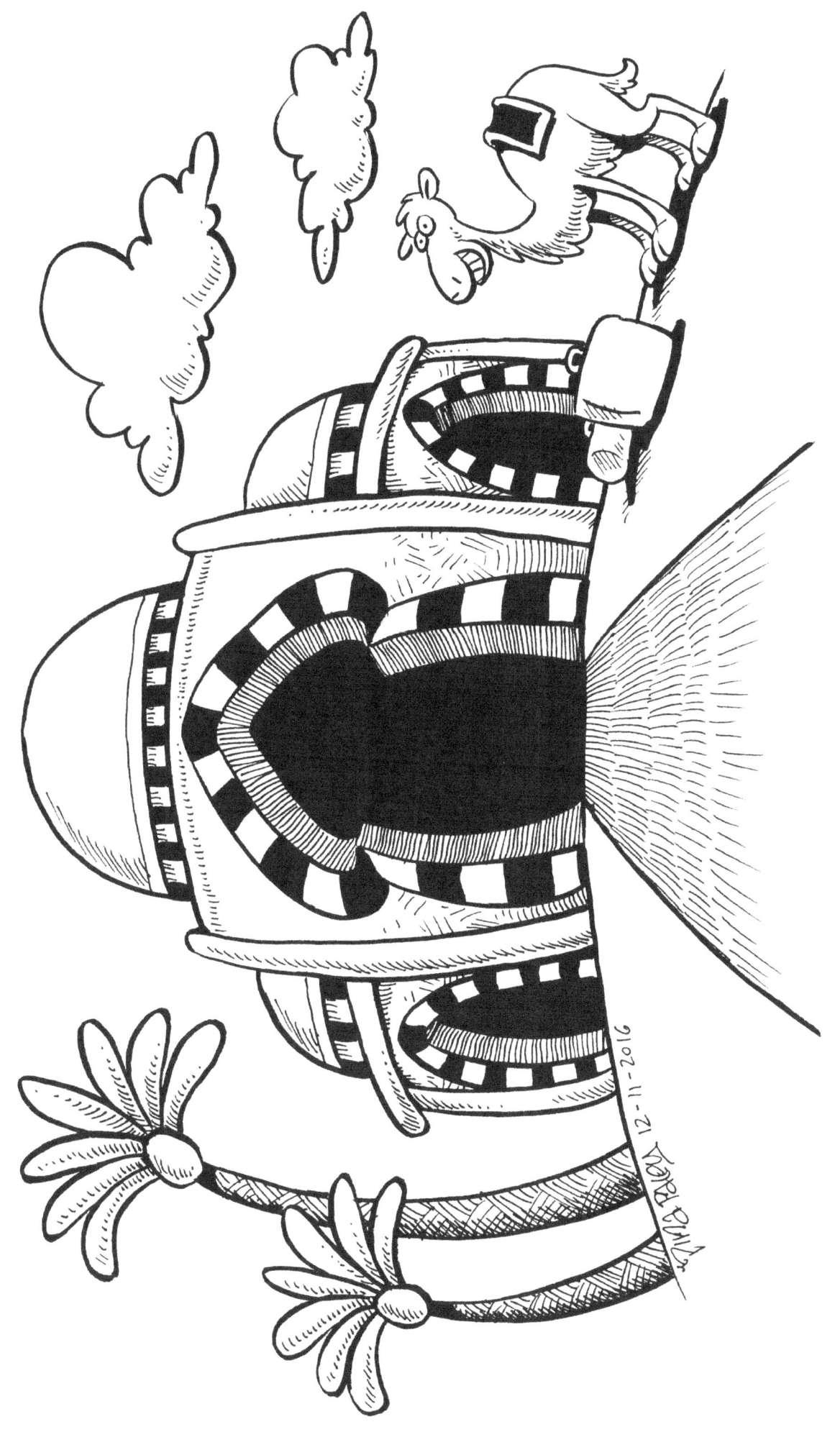

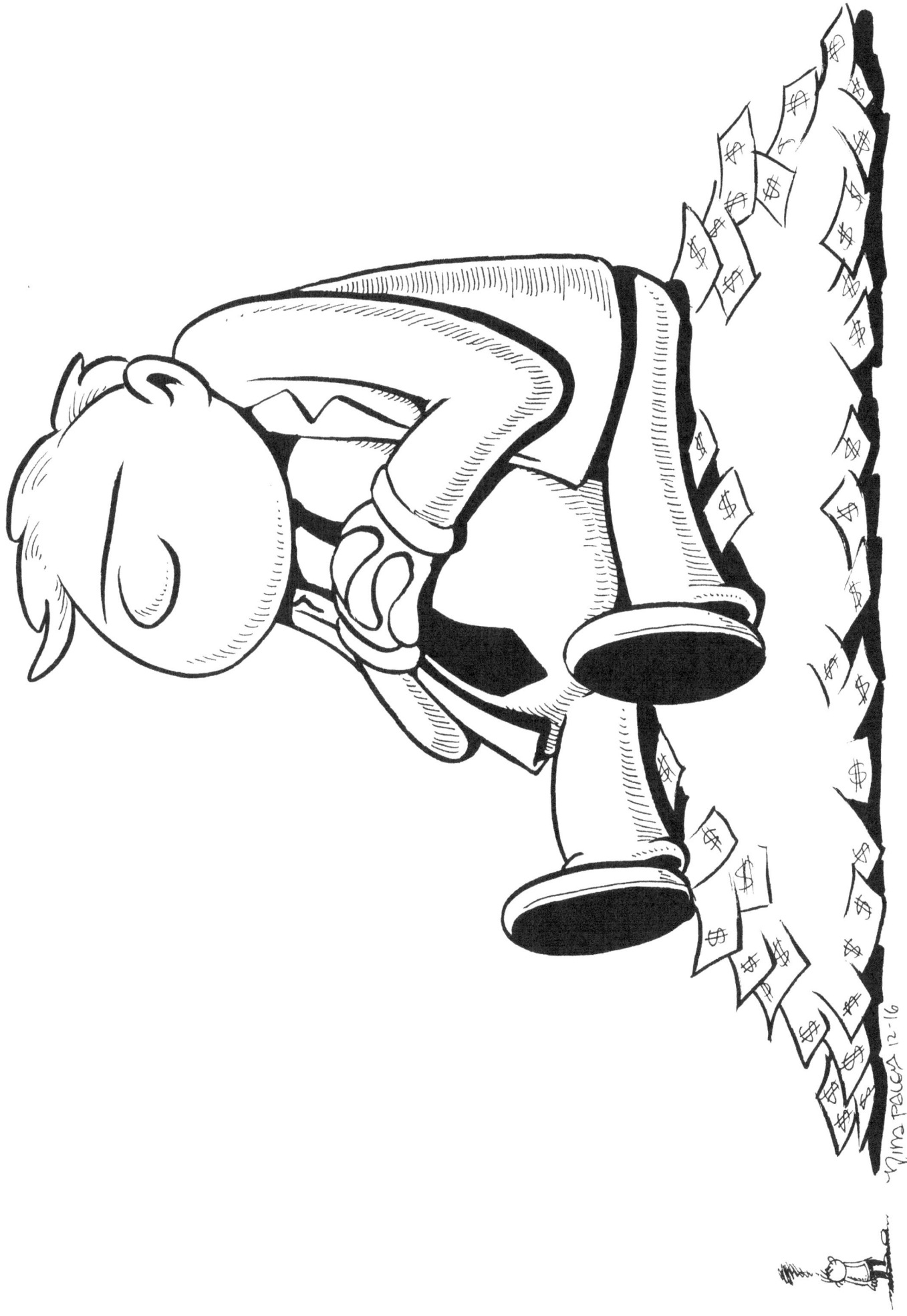

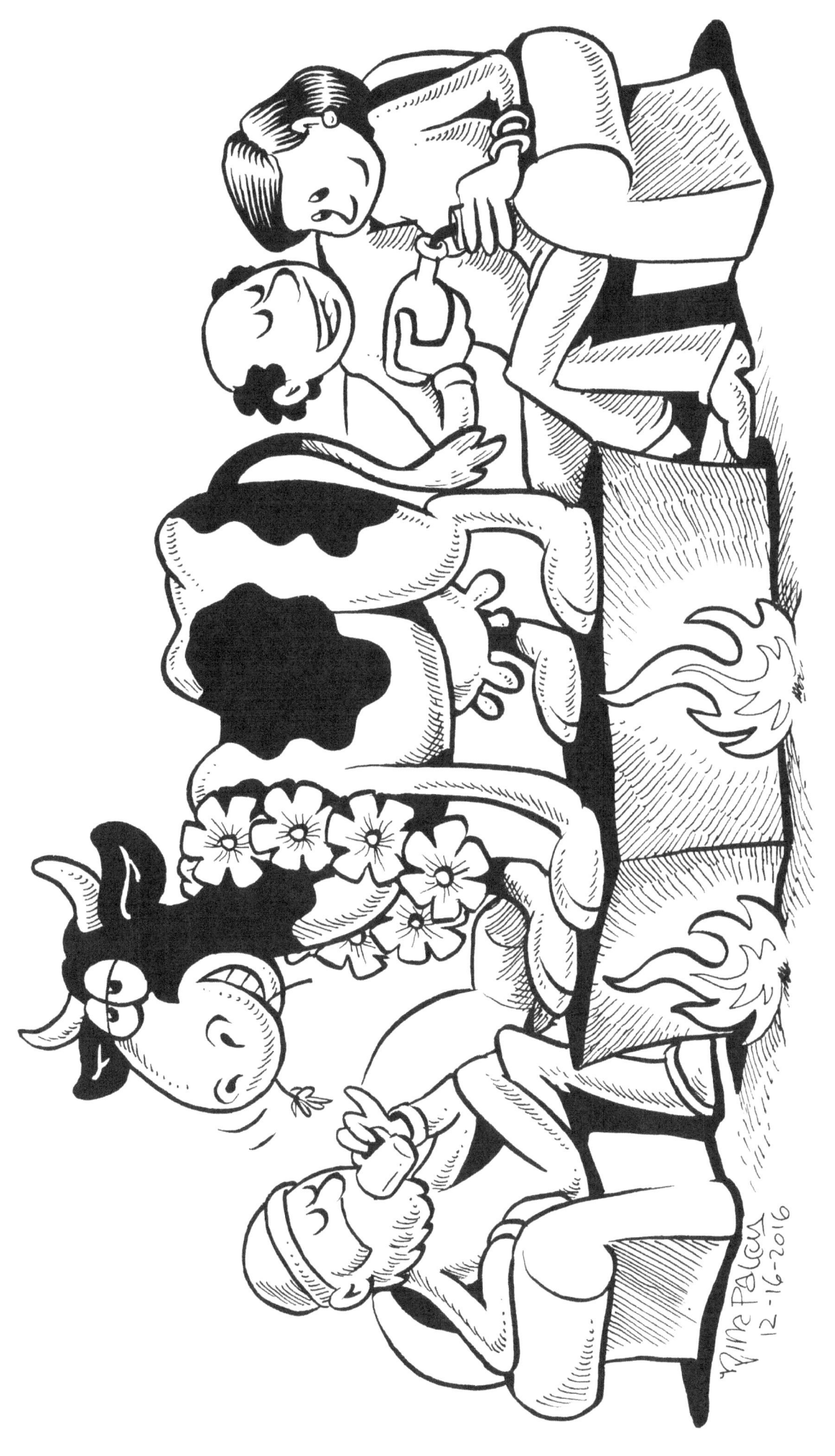

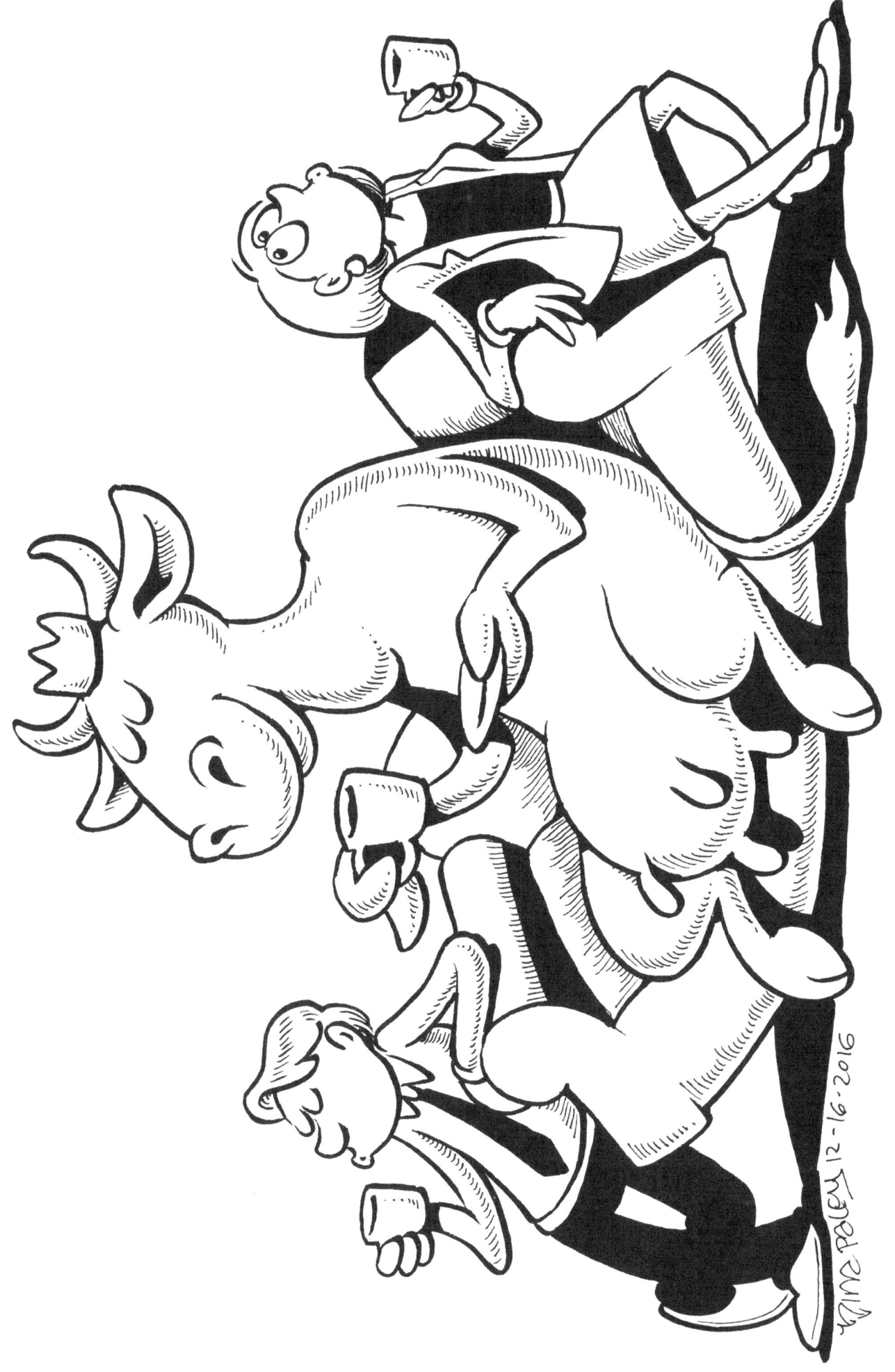

Special Request: "An 800-pound sacred cow in a living room, with a few people ignoring it"
Version 2

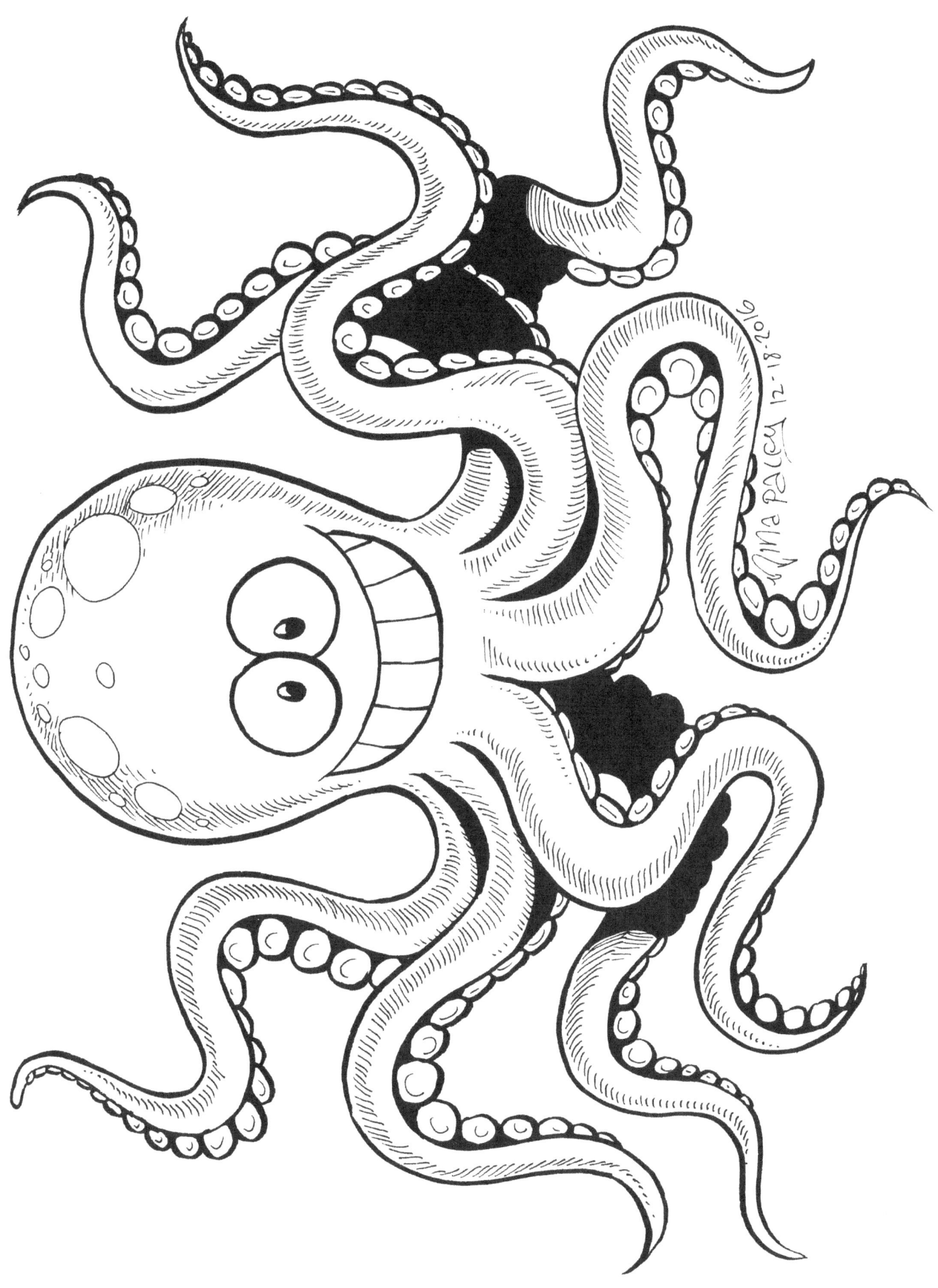

"Amiable Octopus"

www.ingramcontent.com/pod-product-compliance
Lightning Source LLC
Chambersburg PA
CBHW081211180526
45170CB00006B/2298